When a Child Becomes the Four-Year-Old Parent . . .

Trouble Don't Last Always

BY
SHANE SALTER

Copyright © 2006 by Shane Salter

ISBN 0-7414-3695-7

Published by:

INFICOITY
PUBLISHING.COM

1094 New DeHaven Street, Suite 100
West Conshohocken, PA 19428-2713
Info@buybooksontheweb.com
www.buybooksontheweb.com
Toll-free (877) BUY BOOK
Local Phone (610) 941-9999
Fax (610) 941-9959

Printed in the United States of America

Printed on Recycled Paper

Published November 2006

For my mother, grandmother, and great-granddad:
I hope you can now rest knowing that

when I became a four-year-old parent,
trouble did not last always.

Contents

- The national scope of the problem
- Statistics on children and youth in care
- Adult survivors and long-term consequences
- Becoming part of the solution: *CASA for Children*

Acknowledgments

Heavenly Father, the One from whom all my blessings flow, thank you for revealing my life purpose and for never giving up on me as I struggled to understand and to be understood.

Gloria, you are my rock and absolute best friend. Thanks for standing by me, in spite of me. Without you, so many of my dreams would not have come true, and I am eternally grateful. My first daughter, Tiffany, please forgive me for still having some growing up to do while I was raising you. Thank you, David, my oldest son, for teaching me that there is no secret worth keeping. Shane Rico, thank you for giving us a new song to sing, and hang in there, son. Courtney, you're the child my foster mother promised would remind me of what I was like. Thanks for keeping me honest, but I still think some dads *should* take time-outs. My precious daughter, Brittney, just one look at you and the world is all right with me. I adore you for your unwavering love and forgiveness. Moyé, and Nigel, my baby boys, thanks for not putting any more X-men in the toilets. *Lol!*

Mom and Dad Mills, thanks for giving my brother a place to call home and for being there when I needed you most. Pop Moragne, you were the original inspiration for this book. No one really knows when a seed will take root, and when you and Mom opened your home and heart to this kid in crisis, you planted a seed that now bears fruit. Vanessa, you were my guardian angel and never knew it. Pop Cameron, the second time around is so much better. I really appreciate your love and friendship.

Keith, I will always love you. Take it from me: some day we'll all be free. David, Shanique, Omar, Julian, Jacques, Adrienne, Debbie, Satin, and Leroy: keep up the fight and remember our history. Let's make sure it never happens again if we can help it. Dr. Carol Spigner of the University of Pennsylvania, Dr.

Anderson of Michigan State, and Dr. Stewart of the University of Arkansas-Pine Bluff, thank you for stepping out of the box to ensure that emerging social workers gain insight into the complexity of family dynamics, to learn how those dynamics affect children, and to celebrate the wonder of children's resilience. Carol, thanks for the countless times you kept my confidence. You've been like a mother, and thus, a source of comfort to my soul. Dr. Paveo, so many young people have benefited from the gift of your leadership and the generosity of your spirit.

Kolmac, Dr. Michael Richardson, Lonnie, Charles, Jerry, Reese, Alvis, and Joe Carter: thanks for helping me remain true to my conviction that trouble doesn't last always, especially during the Ross betrayal and the following Christmas and New Year holidays. Ron McGowan, now I know that "a friend is someone who sees through your act but still enjoys the show." Valli, through you I learned the purpose for my pain. Your encouragement to go public with my story on the Cathy Hughes radio program opened doors to temporary families for abandoned children and changed my life forever. To my special friend Franklin, I love you, man. Thank you to Rose Dean, Arabella Grayson, Terry Handy, Voni Welch, and Dina Fox—without whom this book would not have made it to print. Special thanks to Nina, Stephen, Nathan, Bill, Nate, Jaiya, and Dwayne for life-long support, encouragement, and contributions to this project. William Bell, Toni Oliver, Jackie Kidd, Wilfred Hamm, Zena Oglesby, Sydney Duncan, Ruth Amerson, Ron Johnson (posthumous), and Joe Kroll: thank you for your support while growing into "my skin" as an advocate. I learned so much from each of you, and it was all different.

Senator Mary Landrieu (D/LA), you have been an unwavering friend and champion for kids. Thanks for more than a decade of support, visionary leadership, and service to our country. Senator Hillary Rodham Clinton (D/N.Y), very early in President Clinton's administration, you asked us to come to the White House to recommend ways to remove the barriers that keep children from finding safe and permanent homes. Thank you for demonstrating that all children in our country matter. It is encouraging to know that New York families have a first-rate advocate in Washington.

Michael Piraino, Eileen McCaffrey, and Carolyn Graham, thank you for your support on my journey of healing from the ultimate professional rejection. Your confidence in me helped me hang on when I almost didn't recognize myself. Tricia Mitchell, Pinkie Mayfield, Curtis Boykin, Dr. Hankerson, John Sampson, Nancy Beams, Bob Guttmann, Sigmund Cohen, Geri Flaum and Crystal Ogene, as co-founders, thank you for supporting the National CASA Association's effort to bring a superior CASA initiative to the nation's capital. Shelvee, Babatunde, Richard, Zachery, Beth, Ursula, and Karl, thanks for your support when others would have given up. To the Board members of CASA for Children of the District of Columbia, your stewardship enables so many of us to realize our mission of keeping children safe.

Dr. Lewis and Mr. Pointer, thank you for listening to Shane, the little boy, when his spirit was dying. You saved my life as a result. Mom and Dad Jenkins, I love you so much. Thank you for all you did to make me what I am and I am not. You were always more than just my foster parents. My life honors you both. Thank you, Mom, for giving me life. I can't wait to see you again.

To those I counted on but who did not show up, I love you anyway.

—Shane Salter

AUTHOR'S NOTE

In some instances, I withheld the names of my foster parents and relatives for privacy's sake. All episodes that appear in this book are real and accurate, and are based on my experience, research, and interviews. This revised edition contains new revelations and captures additional experiences of my evolving journey. It also contains updated resources and additional recommendations for improving the programs and services for at-risk-youth.

The title of this book, *When a Child Becomes the Four-Year-Old Parent... Trouble Don't Last Always,* was inspired by a small choir in Savannah, Georgia, that sang the gospel song "I'm So Glad Trouble Don't Last Always" after I finished a speech to recruit foster and adoptive parents for Georgia children. Although editors, publishers, conference planners and friends have suggested I make the title grammatically correct, I have consistently resisted the pressure to do so and remained faithful to the music in my soul.

Accordingly, you will find that most chapters are introduced by lyrics and titles of music that highlight key aspects of the subsequent experience. Other chapters are introduced by poetry that I wrote over the years while on my journey of survival and healing. I hope, after reading this book, you too will be inspired while remembering that:

> Weeping may endure for a night, but joy
> comes in the morning.
> Keep your faith, it'll be all right, trouble don't
> last always.
> Just stay focused,
> Don't worry about the past.
> Focus on your future,
> Because...trouble don't last.

PREFACE: MESSAGE

You may not know that according to recent estimates, only about one-third of teen mothers go on to receive a high school diploma after having a child, or that among young men who have fathered children, less than half of them go on to complete school, and that even those who do are far less likely to pursue additional education. The grim statistics continue: daughters of teen mothers are 22 percent more likely to become teen mothers themselves, while sons of teen mothers are 13 percent more likely to end up in prison. I determined not to be in that 13 percent.

Motivated by the vision of a better tomorrow, I struggled to be a "loving daddy" and to keep my daughter, Tiffany, from being among that 22 percent statistic. Because the challenge of overcoming generational struggles with teen pregnancy, neglect, and abandonment is so huge, I felt compelled to share with you my journey of meeting that challenge.

I wanted you to know what it was like to be one more baby child born to a teenage mother whose hopes and dreams for her son were shattered by her drug addiction and lack of family support. And, I wanted you to feel what it meant for that little boy to realize that his mother was unable to give him the opportunity to be a child—to grow up in a loving family with a stable home to come back to someday.

This is the story of that boy's journey through the child welfare system, a journey as threatening for a child as any dark alley in America. It is the story of how, with all the odds against him, he survived and emerged more determined than ever to find the dream with his name on it, to succeed and to give back. It is my story, but not mine alone.

It is the journey of hundreds of thousands of children in communities across our country. While each travels alone, we, the grownups, can help them get to a better destination. As I take you down my road, I hope that you will become motivated to think of ways to find your own healing or to help at least one out of the nearly 600,000 children still traveling along this lonely road where childhoods are snatched, spirits are broken, and dreams die. Each year an estimated 20,000 eighteen-year-olds leave the foster care system (the age at which most states relinquish responsibility for those youths) without being adopted or returning to families. I could not escape that statistic. But, nestled inside my story of trouble and triumph—anchored by lyrics of poetry and song—is a message of hope, healing, inspiration, and encouragement, a message that I believe can be heard by the child within each of us.

It is a message aimed particularly at you, my young brothers and sisters. It was with hopes of a better future for you that I took a break from the cares of everyday living to sing my song and remind you that *Trouble Don't Last*. Repeated heartaches and heartbreaks have taught me how hard life can be at times, but with the dawn of each day, I also learned that today does not predict tomorrow, and where you are now isn't where you'll always be. Possibilities for brighter tomorrows begin while dreaming and believing, that "*Change is Gonna Come.*"

A dream is out there with your name on it; find it, and chase it down! When everyone has turned his or her back on you, and your spirit is breaking, dig deep within yourself for strength, stand tall, and remember that tomorrow is a new day. Giving up is never an option. Every experience teaches, prepares, and strengthens. You can't let the pain and heartache from your past move into your heart and start paying rent! Don't ever give anyone the power to kill your dreams or break your spirit.

Yes, we all know many in your situation who didn't make it, who were crushed by challenges passed on through generations. On the other hand, there are many others, and you can be one of those who beat the odds and who get to the finish line by seeking the support and help that is there; reach for it!

As you transition to adulthood, it is important for you to remember that the majority of people in the world aren't interested in whether you were abandoned, abused, or suffered other pain from your past; they just expect you to work it out and function in the present. You must be prepared to show up in school, to show up at work, and to keep showing up! This hard fact is why learning how to reach out and how to get the help you can get, while you can get it, is so crucial. You must work through the pain and break through the prison that keeps you from enjoying meaningful relationships, from obtaining personal success, and from achieving your greatness. Determination feeds the strength you needed to hold on and survive. When pain is no longer your prison, the keys found in forgiveness will begin revealing your life's clear purpose, and doors—too many to count—will begin to unlock. The new freedom from your personal prison enables your dreams to come true. You will then understand what I mean when I sing… "Trouble will come, and trouble will go" … but the one thing about trouble is, "Trouble Don't Last Always!"

To you—all of you individuals and organizations—committed to the lives of children in need, I hope that my journey will strengthen your resolve to open new doors of hope and healing so that a child who feels discouraged by life's troubles discovers his unlimited possibilities. One by one, or through your community organizations or faith institutions, you can demonstrate that every life can be strengthened and every life has value. And you, too, may actualize your life purpose: to make a corner of the world a little better, for the many generations to come

1

One More Baby Child Born

His first look at the world is through a
broken windowpane, beyond that, an alley
leading nowhere. His future is still
unknown, so for the time being ...
he's just one more, baby child born.

—V. Simpson

When I was four years old, I became a parent. Of course, I was too young and too small for the responsibility. My nineteen-year-old mother, Sherry, summoned by her heroin addiction, walked out of our basement apartment in Harlem and left me alone to care for my six-month-old brother, KB. Because I was the older of her two boys, she taught me very early how to prepare bottles and change diapers, and she usually left me in charge when she had to step out. People called me "Little Man," and by default, I was the man of the house. I knew to keep the door locked and never answer it.

On the last day that I saw my mother, her addiction to heroin and alcohol was raging, and once again she left me in charge. How was I to know it would be the last time I was ever going to see her? Why didn't she come back? Did she just give up? Did she want us in the first place? For many years, those unanswered questions tormented me. I was much too young to figure it out then. I could only hope to see her one more time.

Getting through the days and nights without Mom was hard. All I wanted back then was to remain a little boy and a big brother, but the day my mother walked out, I instantly became caretaker and parent. There was no getting around it—I was destined to begin parenthood at age four. By giving me so much responsibility so early, perhaps my mother, without fully understanding it herself, was preparing me for this challenge and for the struggle that lay ahead.

I took care of little KB in the best way a toddler could. How we managed alone remains a mystery to me. The day our mother departed, there was not much in the house left to eat. After a few days, there was no food at all, and I knew I had to go find some. This, necessity, however, meant I would have to disobey my mother. Every time she left us alone, my mom would tell me, *"Never* open the door, *never* leave the house, and *never* let anybody in." Instinctively, I knew I had to ignore her instructions this time, and I headed out the door in search of food, wearing nothing but a dirty diaper.

I can only imagine how sad I must have looked: a filthy, barefoot, four-year-old rummaging through garbage cans for something to eat. I don't know how long I had been searching through the trash when a police officer on foot patrol discovered me. As he approached, I never thought to run. I suppose I wasn't afraid. When he asked me where I lived, I disobeyed my mother again and eagerly led him to our apartment. I should never have let him in, but what was I supposed to do? I tried as long as I could to keep it together while she was away, but I just couldn't any longer, and we really needed help. KB was beginning to cry longer and louder now that we were out of milk. All the food was gone, and Mom still wasn't back. If it had been a fairytale, the story would have ended here, just the way it does on television, with the little boy wearing the police officer's hat and eating an ice cream cone and with everyone living happily ever after. That's not what happened. How was I to know I was getting my mother into trouble? I certainly had no way of knowing that this event was the beginning of the rest of my life without her.

Once the officer was inside the apartment, it was painfully obvious that we had been left unsupervised for more than a few hours. The apartment was filthy and in disarray, and all the food was gone. The police officer had no choice but to call the Bureau of Child Welfare. When the car with the adults arrived to haul KB and me away from our home, I started crying and screaming at the top of my lungs, "I want Sherry! I want Sherry!" I fought and screamed and cried with everything I had to stop them from taking us away, but I finally fell asleep in the car. It's ironic, but I have no recollection of being frightened while at home, even during the times my mother wasn't there; leaving everything that was familiar, however, petrified me.

My next memory is waking up in a new place. Its strangeness made me feel as if I were dreaming. Weird people—fat with bright red lipstick and lots of makeup—were staring at me.

The strange new destination, it turns out, was the downtown location where people processed kids into foster care. Years later, I would learn through that agency's records that I had baffled the caseworkers by repeatedly asking for my brother, Pete. My request puzzled the authorities because they had seen no signs of an additional child on the premises. After my initial intake interview, I underwent a series of evaluations, which included a medical exam to ensure that I had no communicable diseases. My biggest medical problem was severe tooth decay. Because of my mom's lack of prenatal care, I was born with a calcium deficiency that led to a mouth full of rotten teeth and bad breath. Dental hygiene problems notwithstanding, KB and I were deemed healthy enough to be placed in an emergency foster home that night.

Thanks to an attentive police officer and New York City's Bureau of Child Welfare, we had food, a place to sleep, and stability. You would think such comforts would have made me feel safe, but I didn't feel safe at all. In fact, going to my first foster home was traumatic. I didn't want to be in an unfamiliar place with a bunch of strange people; I wanted to be with my mother in our house. It wasn't long after moving in with my first foster family that I became more confused and numb. All my feelings of security vanished, never to return. It was then that I became my only friend and began my fight for survival on this troubled journey.

Just hours after being snatched away from our mother's house, my brother and I arrived at the home of our first foster mother, Miss Fanny. She lived in a New York brownstone just as we had, but unlike my family, she owned hers, and the other occupants in the building were her tenants. She opened her door and ushered us in. I entered hesitantly and walked down the long corridor with apprehension while they placed KB in her arms. The living room was bright and sunny and had a television. Delighted, I immediately ran to it and looked around to see what else was in the room.

Miss Fanny's house was crowded with lots of interesting things that were off limits. I received my orders. "Don't touch this, definitely don't touch that, and under no circumstances are you ever to touch those things," she said emphatically as she pointed to each object. It was overwhelming and impossible for a four-year-old. I wasn't used to so many things in one place because my mom's place was practically bare. The rules were simple—don't touch; sit down; be quiet. But what four-year-old is able to do all that? I couldn't just sit still. I wanted to touch, examine, and play with things, especially the things that were forbidden.

After a few slipups, I suffered the consequences: confinement in the crib that I shared with KB. Because I was small for my age, the two of us comfortably slept together in our very own escape-proof cell. My most vivid memories of our stay with Miss Fanny are of being in the crib and watching a lot of television. It seemed to be on all the time. Television was fine, but why did we have to watch so much of it? Under Miss Fanny's supervision, I got along fine with her children but as soon as she left the house, they stopped being nice to me. It was almost as if someone flipped a switch. Sometimes they would team up and take turns hitting me for no reason at all.

On other days, my fourteen-year-old foster sister would have me all to herself. One day she took me into a room, undressed me, and had me lay face up on the floor. She undressed, too, and gently laid her body on top of mine. She started moving and bouncing up and down on top of me. I don't know how long it lasted, and I didn't know exactly what she was doing, but I remember it made me feel confused and upset. I don't recall how many other encounters there were. Because I didn't know what she was doing or why she was doing it, I never told on her. What was there to tell? I remember my feelings and attitude changed after that, and I became more aggressive. Miss Fanny probably never imagined why I started acting so different.

I passed most of my time at Miss Fanny's in the crib. I hardly ever went outside. Maybe Miss Fanny kept us in the crib all the time to keep me from running around and getting into trouble. I always seemed to be in trouble. If I wasn't pulling and tangling the Scotch tape, I was emptying the salt-and-pepper shakers all over the floor. I was an active little guy who was curious about everything. I wanted to talk and to be talked to. I liked talking—still do! My mother talked to me all the time and answered my questions, but Miss Fanny didn't believe kids should make noise. The old adage, "Kids should been seen and not heard" ranked right up there with the no-touch rule. She kept telling me I talked too much and asked too many questions.

When I wasn't getting into trouble, I was wondering where my mother was and missing her terribly. It would be many years before I understood why my family wasn't able to care for us. It seems odd to me that I understood a lot about the circumstances that forced me to grow up quickly, but much of the foster care stuff would baffle me for years. I knew that I didn't like living with strange people. I knew that I wanted to be with my real family. My memories of living at Miss Fanny's are like being enveloped in fog or a dark cloud. I kept hoping that it would end and that I would wake up in my mother's arms again. I didn't feel as if I belonged there. I felt different from everybody around me and not in a good way. I couldn't express what I was feeling, nor did I realize that children who are separated from their birth parents usually have abandonment and trust issues. No one ever talked to me about what I felt, so I went on pretending I was okay and acting as if I didn't have questions about my family, particularly my mom.

We stayed with Miss Fanny—and I endured the abuse from my foster brother and sister—for about a year while the authorities worked unsuccessfully to reunite us with our mother or to find relatives we could live with. Neither my mom's mother nor her siblings could care for us. Grandma was also a single mother and had five other children, several of them younger than my nineteen-year-old mom. Besides, as I later learned, Grandma didn't want us anyway.

There was no effort to locate my father or anyone on his side of the family. As for my mother, she continued to struggle with alcohol and drugs. It was a battle that cost her everything she had. With her children gone, there wasn't much for her to live for. As her pain grew deeper, there just weren't enough drugs to numb it. Whenever friends or family asked about her sons, and they asked often, she told them we were in Brooklyn with an aunt. That explanation was far better than to hear herself say, "I chose drugs over my kids, and the state took them."

On the day the social worker caught up with her, she was barely able to stand on her feet. She worked hard to pull it together long enough to have a reasonable conversation. The social worker was there on a mission to get Sherry to relinquish voluntarily her parental rights so my brother and I could be adopted. My mother just couldn't let us go. For the longest time, each visit from the social worker ended with the same response, "No." My mother was infamous for her temper, so with each visit the "no" became more animated and the choice words, before and after, a bit harsher. On one of the last visits, my mother slapped the social worker for accusing her of being unfit to parent because she was an addict. I don't know how she got away with that.

A few visits later, Sherry voluntarily relinquished her rights, finally admitting that her children deserved what she could not give them. While all of this was going on, no one ever asked me what I wanted or even talked to me about it. I never even knew she had been found. Why wouldn't my foster mom or my caseworker talk to me about my family? Even at age five, I knew enough to care about the decisions affecting my brother and me. I quickly learned to do what was expected of me, and I kept all my memories, thoughts, and opinions locked inside my head. I didn't ask questions, and I smiled as if everything were okay.

Well, nothing in my life was okay. I could not think of anything but my mother and if she was safe. I knew I was the "Little Man," but living in two worlds was rough.

◆　　◆　　◆

The day I was told we were going to long-term foster care, I recall being extremely afraid, even though I didn't understand what it meant. I remember watching "Speed Racer" and "Gigantor," my favorite cartoons, and telling myself every few minutes "It's going to be okay. Sherry's coming to get us. Yes, Sherry is coming to take us home. She *always* comes back. We're going to be okay." And when this rationale didn't work, I'd start singing some of my favorite songs to make me feel better—at least for a few minutes. I was particularly comforted by the Beatles' song, "Let it Be" in which the lyrics state that Mother Mary comes in time of trouble and whispers words of wisdom and by Simon and Garfunkel's "Mrs. Robinson" in which God blesses her and heaven holds a place for those who pray. I don't know why I developed such a mysterious attachment to those songs at so early an age; maybe they were my mother's favorites too. They continue to bring me a sense of comfort when I hear them even now.

I found no comfort, however, on the morning the officials came to Miss Fanny's door to take us to our long-term foster-care home.

Two very large adults filed in to take KB and me away. They were there to help us, to take us to meet our new foster parents, but I was terrified. I screamed, scratched, bit, and cried hysterically. I held on to the walls, the doors, to anything that I could, to keep them from taking me. I was reminded of that day recently while watching the movie, "Losing Isaiah." In one particularly gut-wrenching scene, Little Isaiah is distraught over being transported from one home to the next. I was Little Isaiah that day. Watching that scene took me right back to the day we left Miss Fanny's, and for just one moment, I was five again experiencing the pain and anguish of it all.

Just like Isaiah, I was defenseless. I could do nothing to stop them from taking us away. I screamed and cried, hoping they would allow us to stay, not so much because I liked living at Miss Fanny's, but because I didn't want to be taken to another strange place where I'd meet new strange people. They eventually managed to put me in the car alongside KB, where I promptly fell asleep, probably from exhaustion.

After a short drive to the Catholic Home Bureau, I was awakened and introduced to a dark-complexioned woman with pearly white teeth. She was wearing a red coat with a matching pillbox hat. Her husband, a tall man with a very light complexion and receding hairline, looked distinguished as he stood beside her with his navy blazer and gray slacks. I could not help noticing he had perfect teeth too. They didn't dress like anyone I'd ever met before. After the formal introductions, I was told that my brother and I were going to be living with them from now on.

2

I Dreamed

I had a dream of days gone by
When hopes were high and life worth
living,
I dreamed love would never die.
Then I dreamed that God would be
forgiving,
But tigers came at night and turned my
dreams to shame.
I won't let life kill the dreams that I
dream.

—A. Franklin

Doris Maxine Jenkins and Robert Louis Jenkins were my new foster parents. They told me that they had a son, Robert Jr., called Robbie, whom we would meet later. He was about three years older than I was, and I was so excited about getting another brother.

They seemed eager to have us join their family, perhaps because my foster father had grown up in an orphanage. Later on, as our relationship grew, he often spoke about his experiences as an orphan during the Depression. He recounted how while living in an orphanage, one morning he closed his eyes to say grace and when he opened them, his oatmeal was gone. After that happened a few times, he started saying grace with his finger firmly in the center of his breakfast. That act stopped it. The story was funny the way he told it, but that visual image made the thought of being in an orphanage unbearable to me. He had promised himself that one day he would give a child the home he had always wanted as a little boy. As the months turned into years with the Jenkins family, I was grateful he'd kept that promise, but I had a hard time adjusting to a new set of parents, a new older brother, and a new set of rules.

When we met at the Catholic Home Bureau, we spent the first few minutes getting acquainted before my brother, KB, and I were led to the Jenkins family car—a very sharp red and white Oldsmobile with wings on the back. As KB and I huddled up next to each other in the back seat, I began to feel overwhelmed by everything. The car seemed so big and I felt so small. I was leaving Miss Fanny and going to live with people we had only just met. I had no idea what awaited us at the Jenkins' house. It was a lot for a five-year-old to process. As we made our way to our new home in Crown Heights, Brooklyn, I remember Mr. Jenkins looking in the rearview mirror and asking me a most interesting question: "What do you want to call us?" Without hesitation, I said, "Mom and Dad." It would be the first time I had ever called anybody Mom and Dad, and from that moment on, that's who they were for KB and me.

When we arrived at our new home, I cautiously scoped out the environment. It was clear to me that this apartment was nothing like any home I had ever seen. It was clean and orderly. The living room had plush, rust-colored carpet, and plastic slipcovers were on the furniture. I had to ask what the big brown wooden thing against the wall was. I'd never seen a piano before. After Dad told me, he said that Robbie took piano lessons and that maybe I might someday too. I had no clue what piano lessons were. The bedroom that KB and I shared with Robbie was light green, brightly lit, and very neat. Everything seemed to have its proper place. I remember thinking, "Boy, oh boy, these people have so many nice things." I wasn't used to all this nice stuff. It was even better than Miss Fanny's place because it was neat and spacious, there was a piano, and all the furniture matched. Then I started to feel scared. I could not keep still or get comfortable. I could not stop thinking about the big men. All I could do was worry whether they would come back to take us away.

We were in a poor state of health when we arrived at the Jenkins. With our calcium deficiency, a condition exacerbated by the fact that my birth mother hated milk, KB's bones were so fragile that, at nearly two years of age, he was still unable to walk. Shortly after our arrival, Mom Jenkins took me to a dentist, who determined that my rotten teeth would have to be extracted to give the permanent teeth a chance to grow in correctly.

By the time I turned six, I had had nine teeth extracted and hideous silver caps placed on the teeth that remained. I thought the caps made me look ugly. They definitely added to my growing sense of feeling different. In an effort to fit in, I would take a safety pin and try to pry them off when no one was looking. One day, I finally succeeded. I ran to Mom Jenkins screaming, "Mom! Mom! Mom! My cap fell off," hoping she would let me leave it off for good. Instead, she promptly took me to the dentist to have it replaced. Boy, did I hate those caps.

On one of our frequent visits to the pediatrician, Mom Jenkins was told that being carried too frequently was as much to blame for my baby brother's fragile bones as the calcium deficiency. People picked KB up constantly because he was such an incredibly handsome little boy. No one seemed to realize that being held so much discouraged him from walking.

◆   ◆   ◆

Robbie, KB, and I shared a room—the other two shared the top and bottom of a high-riser bed, and I had my own folding ottoman. I wanted to share the high riser so I wouldn't be separate. I didn't know why I'd been given my own bed. Was it because I was a bed wetter or because I didn't seem to enjoy being around other kids? In reality, I was self-conscious, insecure, and I desperately wanted to fit in. That mystery was never solved. To make matters worse, my new foster brother, Robbie, was brilliant, was always well behaved, and excelled in school. Much to my dismay, he and KB instantly bonded and became very close. I began to resent both of them.

"Robbie is so smart," everyone would say.

"Isn't KB cute? Just look at those big eyes," others would gush.

People never had much to say about me. My breath always stank because of my rotting teeth, and I had those awful silver caps. My behavior was not the best either. Sandwiched between Robbie and KB, I was lost. I didn't fit in, and no one seemed to notice me. Eventually, I figured out that people paid attention to me when I was in trouble, so I gave them trouble —lots of it.

I started stealing and lying shortly after I arrived at the Jenkins home. The living room was one of my favorite places to hit. Despite having been told on numerous occasions that it was off limits unless an adult was present, I ventured in to take whatever was of real interest to me, especially money. Dad Jenkins used to keep excess change hidden on the top shelf of the bookcase. I remember the rush I would get from taking things that belonged to someone else. The real thrill was in knowing that I usually wasn't caught. Even when I was, the attention I received, however negative, was better than no attention at all.

In addition to thieving, I found myself making up elaborate stories—hoping people would be impressed and listen to me. I really wanted to be heard and noticed. I was so mixed up inside, in so much pain and so confused, that I was willing to do whatever it took to get attention, even if it meant lying.

Mom Jenkins really seemed to like my stories at first. Eventually, however, she and almost everyone else caught on, and no one would believe anything I said. I was branded a liar and a thief, a tag that would follow me throughout school.

♦   ♦   ♦

I started first grade just before my sixth birthday, a considerable accomplishment given all the drama in my life. At St. Francis of Assisi on Lincoln Road in Brooklyn, all eyes seemed to focus on my metallic teeth. To add to my allure, I started wearing glasses. Even I couldn't deny that I looked like a little geek, and my classmates teased me mercilessly. At recess, it was open season, and I became the butt of many a jokester's pranks.

I didn't like myself at all. I was confused and overwhelmed by all the things that were happening in my life. Interacting with kids who lived with their real parents and shared the same last names would get to me from time to time. They all seemed so happy, so perfect. They certainly didn't get into trouble the way I did.

As for my schoolwork, I always hoped the tests would be multiple choice so I wouldn't have to read the question and could randomly select a, b or c. It wasn't that I was lazy; I just couldn't concentrate long enough to read an entire question. Sometimes my multiple-choice method worked, and I got good grades; sometimes I got glaring Ds or Fs, causing my low self-esteem to plummet even further.

To escape, I did what many children in distress do: I daydreamed a lot. I'd drift away and think about my real family: *What are they doing? What do they look like? Do I look like them? Am I that ugly? Why don't they want me? Where is my mother? I wish I could be good; maybe then, people would like me and maybe I would fit in.* These thoughts consumed me and kept me from being a good student.

I found the rigidity and complexity of Catholic school difficult. There were just too many rules, so I tested as many of them as possible to see how much I could get away with. In short order, I became the class clown. The nuns definitely needed some humor in their lives and who better to entertain them than attention-starved Shane.

I thrived on rattling their cages. (I wonder if I'm the only one who ever imagined pulling the habit off a nun's head.) Because of my constant misbehavior, I lived in the principal's office. Sometimes my teacher, Sister Collette, would punish me by making me sit in a trashcan with my legs hanging out. Then she'd add insult to injury by letting other students empty the shavings from their pencil sharpeners on me.

If I wasn't lying or clowning, I was stealing. My parents would give me money to buy books, but I would spend it instead. When I was short on cash, I stole money from my classmates' book bags. Money my parents gave me for my student savings account never made it to the bank because I spent that too.

I thought I was putting it over on everybody, but by the time I got to fourth grade, my reputation as a liar and thief was solidified. I also became known as the kid who couldn't pay attention. My lack of concentration led school administrators to evaluate me for special education classes. No one realized the problem was simply what's commonly known now as Attention Deficit Disorder (ADD). There was little known about ADD then. Fortunately, I was never placed in the special education program, but my struggle to focus on schoolwork and to concentrate continued. As much as I tried to calm my mind and still my body, I couldn't. I knew there was something different about me. Why I couldn't act and think like the other children? Why was I always in trouble?

At every parent-teacher conference, I would overhear my teachers tell Mom Jenkins that I was "not working up to my full potential." That one statement meant extra punishment for not behaving correctly in school. I spent many recesses, timeouts, and afternoons after school standing in the corner facing a wall, angry, confused, or drifting in a daydream. My disruptive, impulsive, and outright aggressive behavior was never associated with a neurological condition that caused my brain to function differently from others. Without the proper diagnosis and intervention, my reputation as "the worst kid in the classroom" gradually changed to being one of the worst kids in the school.

By the time I entered the fifth grade, all the teachers knew that whoever got Shane as a student was in for a challenge, and they treated me accordingly. Sister Miriam Anita, the meanest nun of them all, constantly threatened to have me transferred to public school if I continued to misbehave. Public school was the worst possible punishment that could happen to a kid. The nuns were quick to remind anyone who stepped out of line that public school kids were *mean* and that kids that went to public school got beaten up *all the time*. Public school sounded a lot like Catholic school with me as a lead character, but whenever I heard "the threat," I'd straighten up. I have Sister Miriam Anita to thank for my sporadic good behavior, but even under the threat of expulsion, I would revert to acting out—and not just at school.

Had diagnostic tools and resources for ADD kids been available to me then, my early educational experience could have been very different. I would have been taught how to adapt to the way my brain functioned instead of being pressured to change what couldn't be changed. If my teachers had shown me ways to overcome my learning difficulties and leverage my strengths, I would have been a more confident child and a better student, and I would not have grown up thinking I wasn't good at academics.

The problem was that my brain processes information so rapidly that, while people were talking, I had often gone on to something else. For instance, in math I would often figure out the problem in my head and stop focusing on the remainder of the lesson. Called upon, I frequently gave the correct answer, but got in trouble when I could not adequately explain the steps I took to arrive at my calculation. The "process thing" just does not work for me. I'd bypass one or more steps and race through the equation. Why go to all that trouble if there is a quicker solution? Well, as I would eventually learn, quick solutions do not work for everything in life: I just did not learn that fact in elementary school.

◆   ◆   ◆

During those initial years with the Jenkins family, we would sometimes visit Mr. Jenkins' younger sister, whom we called Aunt Flip. Unlike her older brother, Aunt Flip had very straight hair and looked like a white woman, two traits she took immense pride in. She would tell me the "whiter" I looked and behaved, the more successful I would be in life. She made me pinch my nose so that it wouldn't be so wide. That way, with my "fair" complexion, she thought I could pass for white. Well, my nose is still wide and my skin hasn't lightened over the years, so I guess I won't be passing for white after all. Sorry to disappoint you Aunt Flip.

One day while Aunt Flip was babysitting KB and me at her house, I found some matches and decided to sneak into the downstairs bathroom to play with them. I struck a few of them, tossing them in the toilet bowl to extinguish their tiny flames. Intrigued, I set the toilet paper on fire, which very quickly got out of control. Panicked, I threw the roll into the toilet and a huge cloud of smoke billowed out. I ran upstairs yelling and screaming, with every ounce of conviction I could muster, that my "doo-doo" was on fire, hoping Aunt Flip would actually believe that poop was a highly combustible substance. (I never said I was a good liar.)

When I went home that evening I got my butt torn up. I knew enough to know that foster parents are not supposed to spank children, but the Jenkins treated me as their own. That night, Mr. Jenkins gave me a beating that I will never forget. He said he was beating me out of love and that I would remember that day as long as I lived. Well, he was right. I never forgot how, with every lash of the belt, Mr. Jenkins kept telling me why he was beating me and how much he loved me. From that day forward, I never played with matches again.

My relationship with Dad Jenkins was different from KB's and Robbie's. He had a ferocious temper. I was afraid of him, just as everyone else in the house was, but I really did feel he loved me. He seemed to enjoy spending time with me and talking to me, and we liked to do many of the same things (such as watching "60 Minutes" with Mike Wallace on television). Dad enjoyed teaching me to fix things around the house as much as I enjoyed learning from him. I liked his company and behaved differently when he was around, a fact that didn't go unnoticed by Mom Jenkins. She would often remind me of this split in my personality when I was acting out during his absence. I believe he was the only person in the house who really understood me.

In retrospect, I think I was his favorite in spite of the fact that I was a bad kid. He saw my potential and understood my pain. He'd been abandoned at birth too and had made his way through life without love, support, or nurturing parents. Perhaps he saw a bit of himself in me.

My jealously of Robbie and KB continued to grow throughout elementary school. They were so perfect. Even when they misbehaved, things just seemed to turn out better for them. KB, the cute one and the youngest, floated on a stream of constant compliments and attention. He was smart too, and I hated that. One day while we were running through the house and knowing KB was a few feet behind me, I intentionally slammed a door shut. He crashed into the door so hard that he was knocked unconscious. I was scared when I saw my brother stretched out on the floor. His big lips turned blue, and Mom Jenkins had to use smelling salts to bring him around. Then she knocked the living daylights out of me, and I deserved it.

As if having a real mother and father weren't enough of a reason to resent Robbie, he also turned out to be a child prodigy. He spoke three different languages and played six musical instruments. Unbelievable! I spent many an evening at Carnegie Hall listening to Robbie's musical recitals. Ultimately, my resentment toward Robbie grew to the point of violence. One day, without provocation, I punched him in the stomach as hard as I could. I knew he was soft and would not fight back, so I wasn't surprised when he went crying to Mom. Her response was "If you won't defend yourself, you deserved it."

That statement may have been a good lesson in self-defense for Robbie, but not for an angry, jealous brother. From that day forward, I ruled both my older foster brother and my younger brother, but my satisfaction was fleeting. Stuck between adorable KB and Robbie the genius, shameless Shane was in a difficult situation. The older I got, the worse I felt about myself. I frowned a lot and avoided smiling because of those silver-capped teeth and because Mom Jenkins often told me I smiled like a monkey. Then there were the glasses. Aunt Flip said they made me look like an owl. The other kids thought the glasses had more of a "point-Dexter" mystique and teased me every chance they got. I could not stop wetting the bed no matter how hard I tried, and I was so ashamed. No one liked me, no one understood me, I didn't fit in anywhere, and my caregivers thought I was a monkey-grinning, owl-faced, bedwetting liar and thief. Not a great self-image for anyone, especially a child desperately in need of love. As if I wasn't confused enough puberty kicked in, and Paulette caught my eye. At age thirteen, she was choc-o-late with kinky, rough hair, and I liked it. Paulette lived down the street, and sometimes we'd play house in the stairwell of the six-story building where I lived. That's where she taught me "the nasty." I had no idea my body could feel and do the things it did on the roof that day. It felt good, but I didn't understand what had happened. The excitement of having sex was a little bit scary at first.

Pleasure won out over fear because, soon after my first encounter with Paulette, I tried several times to make myself feel and do those things again. How Mom Jenkins figured out what I was up to in the privacy of the locked bathroom, I'll never know, but one day I overheard her asking Robbie what he thought she should do about my self-discovery.

"Leave him alone; it's normal," Robbie answered. So against her better judgment, she overlooked my indiscretions and never talked to me about them.

As close as I felt to Dad Jenkins, I was uncomfortable talking to him about sex, and going to stern Mom Jenkins was definitely out of the question. While walking home from school, I eventually detoured to the neighborhood library in search of books on human sexuality to help me understand what I was experiencing.

Paulette and I continued our secret rooftop rendezvous, which I never told anyone about. What would they think if they knew I was "doing it" and having all these strange new feelings on top of my behavior problems?

Months later, at a children's Halloween party, I had a different kind of sexual encounter with the host of the party—a white man who lived across the street from us. Midway through the party, he led me to his basement. I remember wondering where everyone was and how I had wound up down there alone with this fat, greasy-looking white man. Then he started touching me all over. I started to run around the chairs, which were scattered about from playing games. I ran up the steps and the door was locked. He called after me. I do not remember exactly what he said, but it was something along the lines of "big boys don't run," and then he unlocked the door and I ran home.

Another time, while I was playing in front of my building, the same man offered me potato chips if I'd let him touch me again. I like chips but did not get in the car that time. Just looking at him made me sick. I later learned he had molested another child in the neighborhood. Even though I never told Mom and Dad Jenkins about the incidents, I was fortunate to have an adult in my life in whom I felt comfortable confiding, Dr. Lewis—a therapist whom I had started when I was nine. She listened and reassured me that it was not my fault and that I had done nothing wrong. It wasn't until I became an advocate for children that I learned the alarming statistics on child molestation: One out of every four girls and one out of every five boys is molested before reaching the age of eighteen.

◆   ◆   ◆

Like most kids my age, I wanted to have my own pocket money, and I was lucky enough to get a paper route. The pay was good, and the tips were great. I'd been on the job for a few weeks when one day, on one of my regular stops, I rang the front doorbell and no one answered. I turned the knob and the door opened. A pair of pants was hanging over a chair, and I couldn't resist pushing the door all the way open, sneaking inside, and going through the pockets. I left the newspaper (as evidence, of course) and raced out of the apartment. I don't remember how much money I got, but I felt rich. It was like Christmas in July. I went down the street to the store and bought a tape recorder and a bunch of other things.

When I got home and Mom Jenkins saw my new purchases, she correctly deduced that I had stolen the money and was convinced I had taken it from her purse. Dad Jenkins also thought that I had stolen the money, but from his stash in the living room. *What hypocrites*, I thought. Here they were chastising me for stealing, and both of them were trying to claim something that did not belong to either of them. It never dawned on me that there might be another thief in our midst. Was I the only Jenkins boy with sticky fingers? I thought Prince KB and Sir Robbie would never stoop so low. I listened in silence as my accusers argued over whose money had been lifted. If they knew where I had really gotten it from, it would have made the situation worse, so I never said a word.

Confused, distressed, and plagued by trouble, I concluded that the best solution for my problems was to run away. The next Sunday morning, I took all of my paper route tips and my newly acquired loot, hooked up with my friend Stacey who lived downstairs, and took off. We thought we were set, but the money ran out after our first stop at White Castle for hamburgers and fries. He'd barely licked the grease from his lips when he punked out and went back home. I didn't want to go back home, but I did. Less than two hours on the road and I was back home. No one even knew I was AWOL.

I gradually grew so unhappy there that I felt as if I couldn't do anything right and that no one liked me. Even Dad Jenkins' patience was wearing thin. I was eleven years old and had been seeing a therapist for two years, but therapy didn't help me improve my self-image: it made me feel even more different from my brothers and classmates. As my self-esteem fell, my behavior worsened. I told Dr. Lewis about my loneliness and the deep hole that losing my mother had left in my heart. That pain was still strong, even though I thought less and less about seeing her again as time went on.

My arrival at the Jenkins home triggered daydreams of adoption and of sharing their surname. I thought that change might fill the emptiness inside me. For some reason, the thought of signing my name "Shane Jenkins" was the most appealing part of it. I wanted to belong to someone, to fit in. If I had the same name as the family I lived with, people wouldn't be able to tell from my name that I was different.

My therapist told me that adoption was permanent, and if Mom and Dad Jenkins adopted us, KB and I would be secure forever. No more sudden moves, no more strange people. In one of my therapy sessions, I wrote a three-page play called "The Adopted Child" in which the Jenkins family adopted me. In the end, that's all it was, a play.

KB and I lived in the Jenkins home for more than seven years, and we were given the best of everything. We were nurtured, disciplined, and humbled and were given lots of love, private educations, and the finest clothing. Never did they treat us any different from their birth son. We even dressed in matching clothing, as if we were triplets. We went to the same private schools, got the same medical care, and shared the same room.

Nevertheless, I always knew I was different. I didn't talk about it, but I knew my name was Salter and theirs was Jenkins. Every time I had to write my name on a school paper or went to the doctor and she called me by my last name, I was reminded that I didn't really belong.

◆   ◆   ◆

During our seventh year with the Jenkins family, my social worker told me that my brother and I would be moving from our long-term foster care placement to an adoptive home soon. I don't remember anyone explaining to us why we couldn't be adopted by the Jenkins. I didn't ask. I just assumed that I was too much trouble. I wasn't in a good place no matter how hard I tried to pretend. Why didn't I think it was okay under the circumstances to be confused, hurt, and angry? Quietly to myself and alone in my mind, I retaliated.

So what if they don't want me? I'm going to get my own family anyway. Maybe my new family will even think I'm cute. I hope I can stop being so much trouble; maybe then they'll love me forever. But my first question upon hearing the news was, "Will my name be the same as my new parents?*"*

"Yes, Shane," Mr. Pointer said.

I was ecstatic.

Because of our advanced ages, KB and I were classified as "hard to place." In most states, children aged eighteen months and older are deemed hard to place because babies are considered more desirable, adapt better, and exhibit fewer abandonment issues. Because we were black and came as a package, our chances of getting a good permanent home were decreased further. For a fleeting moment, I wished I didn't have a brother. Maybe then my chances would be better. Maybe people wouldn't compare me to him and talk about how cute he was all the time. However, in reality, my brother was my world. We were joined at the hip. I wouldn't go anywhere without him or ever leave him behind.

The recruitment process to find the best adoptive family moved very quickly after our photographs appeared in the *Amsterdam News.* I barely recognize the description of myself, even with the fictitious name:

> Aside from being a very handsome-looking,
> bright and creative young man, Sean loves singing
> and dancing and writing plays. He has a warm,
> outgoing personality, a good wit, and is delightful
> company. He also makes friends easily once he
> gets to know you and has very little difficulty in
> relating to friendly adults. That's because he says,
> "I like people.

When "advertising" for adoptive families, it is common practice for agencies to give children fictitious names for privacy, but somehow KB's real name made it into print.

Amsterdam News - 1976

Sean and Keith

Sean And Keith:
An Adoptable Duo

Recently Sean, a 12-year old, was awarded a silver medal of honor for helping to rescue a baby from a fire. "And why not," says Sean, he goes on to say, "after all I'm a Boy Scout."

Having demonstrated such a remarkable act of courage and bravery, Sean and his nine year old brother, Kenneth are in need of an adoptive family as soon as possible. Especially a loving family who can provide a stable, secure and permanent home for them. One in which they can be very proud of knowing that someone willingly opened their home to them which they justly deserve.

Aside from being a very handsome looking, bright and creative young fellow, Sean loves singing and dancing and writing plays. He has a warm, outgoing personality, a good wit and is delightful company. He also makes friends easily once he gets to know you and has very little difficulty in relating to friendly adults. That's because he says, "I like people."

Sean and Kenneth have been a foster home for seven years which they thoroughly enjoyed and were made to feel an integral party of this family. Though the foster family agreed to care for them temporarily until a permanent home could be secured.

Due to their earlier life experience of being separated from their own family, one can imagine how painful and difficult it must be for them. That is, to miss out on the love that only a mother can give a child.

In spite of his good looks and unique sense of humor, Kenneth for the most part wears a bright smile and sports a "mischievous twinkle" in his eyes. Yet, he's so very affectionate when caught off guard. This doesn't imply that Kenneth is a "mommy's" boy, but he likes a hug every now and then to assure him that he's loved. In his spare time, Kenneth enjoys drawing but most of his energy is used in "hard play."

Sean and Kenneth would do well with a family who really want and need them. For more information on adopting these boys and other children like them, please contact the Adoption Department of Catholic Home Bureau, 1011 First Avenue New York, N.Y. 10022-tel. (212) 371-1000 ext. 370.

Several families responded to the newspaper article, and eventually the most suitable family was selected. Eager to have a permanent home, I was determined to be on my best behavior. If I could be perfect, someone would finally want me and love me. I got the feeling that our new parents wanted me to be perfect too.

During the pre-placement weekend visits, there always seemed to be much excitement over our impending arrival. We were given everything we wanted. There seemed to be no limit to our new parents' generosity and kindness. A steady stream of relatives came by the house to meet us, or we drove to their homes to meet our prospective new grandparents, aunts, uncles, and cousins. We were introduced as the latest addition to the family, and it was great getting all of the attention and repeatedly hearing how handsome both KB and I were. A few relatives even commented on "the strong family resemblance."

On one particular visit, when Mr. Pointer, our social worker, dropped us off, he asked our soon-to-be parents when they would bring us back. Our new Dad's response was "the twelfth of never." *How's that for having a real home and family? Our names will be the same as theirs. My dream is coming true: I will have a real family of my own, a place where I belong.* We finally had it made.

With "the twelfth of never" still ringing in my ears, I went back to the Jenkins home confident and obnoxious in the belief that my turn had finally come. Not only was I going to be moving in with a new family, but they were also rich. I was moving up in the world—going from an apartment in Crown Heights, Brooklyn, to a townhouse duplex in Co-Op City in the Bronx.

Nonetheless, I was angry with Mom and Dad Jenkins for not adopting us. They never discussed their reasons with us and we never asked. Because no one told me why my foster parents wouldn't adopt me, I told myself I would show them that their rejection didn't matter to me. I danced around the house making up songs with words intended to hurt my foster family. "I'm so glad I'm leaving, because I'm going to a new home where people will love me forever." With each verse, I kept getting louder and louder to be sure that everybody in the house heard me clearly; that way they wouldn't know that deep inside I felt rejected, scared, and lonely. Once the paperwork was finalized, I really started acting out. A part of me really didn't want to leave what was familiar and safe. I didn't want to start all over again with another set of parents, a new set of rules, a new school, and a new set of friends. I wasn't sure how well I'd adapt.

Then there was part of me that looked forward to the new beginning, a chance to start all over again. I hoped the new people would understand me. I wanted to try, but I wasn't sure I could hold up my end of the bargain. Also, adoption was a new option for us, and I didn't know the rules of the game.

I don't know if the Jenkins family ever knew how conflicted I was because I went out of my way to act as if I were happy to be leaving, but my act was short-lived and probably about as convincing as one of my most transparent lies.

A few short weeks of my boastful indifference and feigned happiness abruptly ended the day KB and I left the Jenkins home for good. We were finally being adopted. It should have been the happiest day of my life, but I cried and cried and cried.

"Mom, I don't want to go," I sobbed, hugging her as tight as I could. "Please Mom, please."

My foster brother Robbie started crying too. I didn't think he even liked me. Why was he crying? *He gets to have his parents all to himself*, I thought. But when he hugged me and said good bye, I knew it was real.

I looked up at Mom and Dad, and they were crying too. Why? I thought they wanted us to go. Mom Jenkins never showed much affection, but at this moment, she held me and said, "You'll be okay, son."

She tried her best to put a positive face on things. "You've got a new family waiting for you and KB. Be good," she said, "And remember, we love you. The Robertses will take good care of you and KB. You wait and see. You'll forget all about us after a while."

"No, Mommy," I wailed. "I'll never forget you; I promise."

We hugged, and I continued to cry uncontrollably.

"Don't let me go," I pleaded.

She just pushed me away.

"It's time, son," Dad Jenkins said.

"No. No!" I screamed.

I grabbed KB, and the waiting adults grabbed me.

My instinct was to fight as hard as I could to stop them from taking me away. Suddenly, I surrendered. I didn't scream, scratch, kick, or bite. I took KB by the hand and let them lead us outside to the waiting car. As we drove away, I wiped my eyes and thought about my new life and how wonderful this new family was going to be.

3

A Family

When you look in my eyes,
Do you see
A little boy
Wanting to be
Loved by a family?
When you look at my face
With no shame or disgrace,
Please remember
I'm just trying to run this race.
I'm trying to be
What I'd wish you'd see:
A boy who's a part of your family.
Oh, what I'd do
If I could start anew
And rest among the chosen few.
You see,
I'd cry no more tears
For the yesteryears,
But I'd smile with joy
For the little boy
Who became a part of your family.

—S. Salter

When we arrived at our new adoptive home, the Robertses were excited to see us. Mr. Roberts worked for the Port Authority as a bus driver, and Mrs. Roberts was a photographer and a beautician. She was a fox. They had one son named Anthony. Anthony saw our pictures in the *Amsterdam News* and begged his parents to let him have two brothers. On our absolute best behavior, we tried to behave like two model foster children. Everything in the article seemed to be as stated. KB and I were okay kids. Things were going really well, but a month after our arrival, the honeymoon ended.

During the pre-placement visits, Anthony and I got along great, but as soon as we moved in, he became resentful. I guess he thought having brothers would be a lot more fun than being an only child, but he soon learned that having two brothers meant sharing space, food, and his parents' attention. We would fight a lot about seconds at the dinner table. I think he was all right with sharing attention and living space, but he was big, and his eating less was out of the question.

We would also fight over the pettiest nonsense whenever Mr. and Mrs. Roberts weren't home. We would chase each other through the house with the rage of mortal enemies determined to fight to the death. I was usually the one who picked up a stick. I wanted to beat him upside his head every chance I could get. I never could though. Anthony was no Robbie. He was a football player, and he could fight. I wasn't used to that. He would wrestle me down or body-slam me once he caught me. When I lost a fight to Anthony—and I usually did—I would run to the closest pay phone and call Mom Jenkins to complain and cry. I would tell her that I missed all of them and wanted to come back home.

Without fail and with incredible clarity, Mom Jenkins would painfully remind me that the Robertses were my family now and that KB and I could never come back to live with her, Robbie, and Dad Jenkins. "You got to make this work, Shane," she would say.

"But I'd rather live with you."

"You have a permanent home and a family that will adopt you. You have a new life now," she would remind me.

I'd hang up disappointed but motivated to try to get along with Anthony and to stay out of trouble.

There were things that I liked about the Robertses. They were much younger than Mom and Dad Jenkins, and their house was bigger. Because Mrs. Roberts was a photographer, I took an interest in photography, and they bought me my first camera. All my friends thought my new Mom was cool too. It didn't take long before I started making friends in my new neighborhood.

I really hit it off with Todd, a tall, smooth-talking guy with curly hair; all the girls were crazy about him. I thought Todd's single mom was so cool because she would often go out on dates, giving Todd and me chance to get into all kinds of mischief.

One of my favorite neighborhood friends was a gorgeous Jamaican girl named Carmen. Man, was she hot. We would exchange notes and an occasional kiss when we passed one another in the hallways of the apartment building. One day, I got her to agree to skip school and go home with me. We got to the house, went to my room, got out of our clothes, and started to have sex. Just as things were steaming up, my foster mom came home and caught us. She screamed and told us to put our clothes on. That's when my real trouble began.

Of course, Mrs. Roberts told Mr. Roberts what I had done.

"Shane, I'm extremely disappointed in you. Not only have you tarnished the reputation of this family, but also, you have compromised the reputation of that girl and her family. I won't tolerate that kind of behavior in my house again. Do you hear me? I'm beginning to believe you can't be trusted to do what's expected of you." He was furious.

Although I pleaded with her not to, Mrs. Roberts telephoned Carmen's parents and told them what we had done. Carmen's parents punished her by beating her terribly with an extension cord and forbidding her from speaking to me ever again.

After I told Todd about the incident, it didn't take long for the news to spread. Everyone at school was talking about the fact that we were caught, which, ironically, made me more popular. I was now running neck and neck with Todd for the title of coolest dude in school because everyone knew I was getting my groove on with the girls.

After a week or so of being in the doghouse at home and having every privilege taken away, I started to feel that I wasn't good enough to be a member of this family. My lying, stealing, and bedwetting increased. Then one day my whole world came to a screeching halt.

KB and I had been living with our new family for only about two months when my social worker, Mr. Pointer, unexpectedly made a visit to my school. I was called out of homeroom and told to report to the main office. As soon as I entered, my heart stopped. Mr. Pointer was standing at the counter waiting with a sad look on his face.

"We need to talk, Shane," he said as he led me back into the hallway. "The Robertses called."

I immediately thought, "Oh, oh." I knew enough to know that his referring to them as "the Robertses" instead of "your parents" was a bad omen.

"Things are not working out as they had hoped," he went on to say. "They want you and KB to leave."

I couldn't believe it.

"How long before we have to leave?" I struggled to get the words out. With no detectable show of emotion, he responded, "Tomorrow."

I was struck by lightning, and my fragile heart was fried. It didn't seem to matter that I would turn thirteen in a few days or that we had made plans to celebrate Thanksgiving as a family. In fact, no one seemed to mention it. I was crumbling but couldn't move. All the hope and trust I had placed in so many adults—adults who kept letting me go, passing me off—died as I leaned against the wall in that hallway. The wall was my tower of strength. Sherry,

Miss Fanny, Mom and Dad Jenkins, a host of nameless adults working in the foster care system, my teachers, the nuns, none of them could save me from yet another set of parents who were sending us back. It felt as if we were cargo with a stamp "Return to Sender." I would never trust again, and I would never believe the words "I love you." I went numb. I retreated to that dark blanket of fog and confusion. They killed the spirit of that little boy who so desperately wanted love and acceptance. My childhood innocence was snatched away forever during that ten-minute conversation with Mr. Pointer.

"Mr. Pointer, why? Why don't they want me? Do adults ever mean what they say?" I asked, fighting back the tears as a new sense of rage welled up inside me.

"I thought they meant it when they said 'the twelfth of never.' Even the shrink said adoption was permanent; so what happened? What did I do that was so terrible?"

Mr. Pointer tried to console me as best he could.

"Shane, you and KB will be okay," he said.

"Okay, Mr. Pointer? Okay?" I repeated, my voice rising. "What did I do that was so terrible? Tell me what I did? Where am I going to go?"

He quietly and calmly explained that KB and I would be going to an emergency foster home in the South Bronx. We were going to be moving from the somewhat upscale Co-Op City to a housing project in the area where I was born. I knew it would be rough. "Couldn't you find any place better than that?" I complained.

I told Mr. Pointer I needed to say good-bye to my friend before I left because this would be my last day at that school. I couldn't leave without saying good-bye to Todd. I found him after school hanging out in the park. I told him that I was going to be moving away the next day. He was shocked when I told him that I was a foster child and the Robertses were not my real parents.

"My name really isn't Shane Roberts. It's Shane Salter," I revealed.

"Man, stop lying. Why are you messing with me like that?" he said. When he realized I wasn't kidding, I could see a real sadness in his face. Then he asked me where I was going.

"I don't really know, Todd. They tell me it's a family in the South Bronx," I said, as tears began to roll down my cheeks.

Todd tried his best to console me. "Don't cry, Shane. We'll stay in touch. You'll still be living in the Bronx," he pointed out.

"Maybe I can come visit sometimes," I said.

My next task was to tell my brother KB that we were going to have to leave yet another home. Just like me, I knew he really wanted this adoption to work. How could I break his heart by telling him that the Robertses wanted us to leave? I found him in our bedroom listening to Natalie Cole's, "Good Morning Heartache." How ironic. "Hey, KB. I need to talk to you. It's important. I'm sorry, but we have to leave the Robertses. Mr. Pointer is coming to get us tomorrow," I told him.

"Why? They don't want us anymore?" He looked as sad and confused as I had only hours earlier.

"Don't worry, little brother; we're going to be okay."

I didn't have a clue what "being okay" really meant. Because the adults around me always said that whenever I was moving to another home, that's what I told KB. He didn't know what "being okay" meant either.

That night as we started to pack, I heard my soon-to-be-ex dad come in the house. A few minutes later, I went into his room to beg him not to send us back. Nothing I said seemed to change his mind.

"Shane, you created this situation. It's your fault that things didn't work out. You and KB have disrupted this family long enough.

It's time for you to leave. This has been a difficult time for us. I almost lost my wife once," he went on to say, "and I'm not going to let anyone or anything come between us again."

I fell on my knees crying and begging, "Please, Dad, don't send us back."

"Shane, it's too late. The decision has been made. Now go back to your room and finish packing."

Through the heartbreak, I mustered up the strength to tell myself I could handle whatever situation we might have to deal with in our emergency foster home. I was twelve, but what about KB? I was very worried about him. He understood far less than I did. Now that I was back to being his parent again, I needed to find a way to comfort him—to reassure him—but all I could do was apologize.

"I'm sorry, KB, I'm so sorry."

I finished our packing and went to bed.

Maybe they will change their minds by tomorrow, I thought.

When I awoke the next morning, my head seemed cloudy, and I was overwhelmed with an incredible aloneness. I felt like the unwanted, motherless child I was.

Of course, the Robertses had not changed their minds, and Mr. Pointer did not pick us up. Our ex-parents placed our belongings and us in the car and drove very fast to the agency. During the entire ride, they kept saying the same thing over and over.

"You blew it, Shane. You blew a perfectly good home and family who loved you.

Under my breath I mumbled, "If you really love us, why are you giving us back?"

"As long as you continue lying, stealing, and wetting the bed, you will never have a good home," Mr. Roberts declared.

That car ride and their loud voices will be forever etched in my mind. I couldn't see or hear anything else. It was like a bad dream. To make matters worse, when we pulled up in front of the foster care agency at 1011 First Avenue, the Robertses pulled us from the car, dumped us on the curb, and sped away. KB and I were left standing all alone with our clothes in garbage bags. We looked at each other for a minute, and then I took KB's hand and walked with him into the lobby of the huge forty-story office building.

I told the security guard seated in the lobby at the front desk who we were and what had just happened. He went back outside with us to retrieve our clothes, and after asking which agency we belonged to, he called someone from the Catholic Home Bureau, and we were escorted upstairs. Right away, we were told about the next family we would be living with: a Mr. and Mrs. Balfour.

While we waited to be taken to the Balfour home, I made a decision not to steal from people anymore. As I saw it, the new foster home was another chance for a new beginning. No one had to know anything about my past unless I told them about it or showed them. I didn't want to be known as a liar and a thief anymore. I didn't want people hiding their purses and wallets and talking about me behind my back. I couldn't handle that baggage anymore, not with everything else. I was no longer going to let my bad behavior prevent me from getting ahead. I wanted it gone. If it was going to stop me from getting a home, I wanted it gone. As of that day, anything that was going to stop me from reaching my dreams was *gone*—whatever it took. Nothing and no one was ever going to say again that *I* was the reason holding me back.

Private transportation was arranged for our trip from Manhattan to the Bronx. The Balfours lived in the Moore Housing Project on 149th Street in the South Bronx. The building didn't look so bad from the outside, but as soon as we got into the elevator, the stench of urine was so strong I almost passed out. I had to catch my breath. Going from the Jenkinses' upscale apartment, to the Robertses' beautiful townhouse, to the projects in the South Bronx was unreal. I tried not to walk in the apartment building with a bad attitude. I was grateful for having a place to stay. *Shoot,* I had just been kicked out of somebody's house with my little brother—but was this really where we were going to be living?

I pretended, for the sake of Mr. Pointer, as if I didn't smell the weed when we walked into the lobby, but the pungent odor of urine was just outright nasty. Thank God, our new foster care mother lived on the fourth floor so the elevator ride didn't last long. As I got on the elevator, I was wondering what Mr. Pointer must be thinking. Would he live here? Whatever his thoughts were, he kept them to himself.

A tall woman wearing a twisted wig and crooked glasses answered his knock. I stood there in disbelief. *This can't be happening*, I thought.

"Come on in," she said.

Oh, no, I thought.

I was hoping she would say something more along the lines of "I'm sorry, but you obviously have the wrong apartment."

No such luck. I considered my options as she and my social worker chattered away. *Just tell me I get to register my own self for school. That is all I want to hear. I promise I'll get the best grades, if you promise never to show up at my school.*

The apartment was dreary and had the distinction of being the first roach-infested place I had ever lived. I wanted to run back to the Jenkinses' house, but I couldn't. This was going to be my home now, and there was nothing I could do about it. There weren't a whole lot of options for two kids our ages. The Balfours were natives of the Virgin Islands with two grown children living elsewhere, and they were considered "professional" foster parents. Countless foster children had come in and out of their door, including one they had adopted permanently: Anthony, a kid about my age. Our status was clear from the outset. Mr. and Mrs. Balfour were not going to treat KB and me as well as they treated their adopted son. I guess the underlying message was "Don't get too comfortable, you won't be here that long." Anthony went to Catholic school. KB and I were enrolled in a nearby public school. Anthony had his own room. KB and I shared one. All of the candy, cookies, and other goodies were locked up in the hallway closet. Anthony had the key. We didn't. It was without question his home and not ours.

We moved in with the Balfours during the holiday season. I was really looking forward to a Christmas like the ones we had with the Jenkinses, with a tree and a living room filled with neatly wrapped presents. However, KB and I awoke on Christmas morning to find not one thing under the tree for us. Mrs. Balfour said that we came a little too late for her to get us anything.

"I do my Christmas shopping during the summer when prices are low," she explained.

At first, I thought she was joking, but she was dead serious. My brother and I just stared at each other. What did we do to deserve this? Wasn't it bad enough that my birthday, which was just past on November 21, had been ruined?

I saw my therapist, Dr. Lewis, a lot more frequently during my stay with the Balfours. During one visit in March, I had an experience that would change my life. The receptionist at the Catholic Home Bureau noticed that my last name was the same as that of a woman sitting in the reception area. Out of curiosity, she asked the woman if she knew a Shane and KB Salter. Well, not only did she know us, she said that we were her grandchildren!

When I arrived for my appointment a few minutes later, the receptionist grabbed me as soon as I got off the elevator.

"Shane, Shane, your grandmother is here!"

"What?" I inquired, completely puzzled.

I didn't know what to think because I had never met my grandmother. No one had ever talked to me about her, and she wasn't a part of any of my childhood memories.

I was confused and nervous as the receptionist led me to a short, plump woman who stood up and said, "Shane, I'm your grandmother. And this is your sister," she said, pointing to the toddler standing beside her.

Shocked and elated, I hugged my grandmother, sinking happily into her soft bosom. It was the most comforting and sincere hug I had ever experienced. It seemed so real, so natural, and so right. Memories of my early childhood came flooding back, and so did the unanswered questions about all those years.

"Do I have a brother named Peter?" I asked.

"No, but you have an uncle who is only six years older than you named Pierre," she said.

"I remember him, Grandma, I remember him! All these years, I thought he was my brother. We must have spent a lot of time together."

"You sure did, Shane," she confirmed.

I once thought my grandmother was a dark, thin, silver-haired woman with a Caribbean accent who used to feed me lots of red rice, and I asked her who that woman was.

"Oh, that's Ms. Turner; she was a sweet lady who lived in our building. She used to babysit you."

I was so excited that I was practically babbling now. "I remember the building I lived in; it had yellow brick and a fire escape outside the window."

She seemed genuinely impressed and shocked by how much I remembered.

Meanwhile, Mr. Pointer called the receptionist to ask if I had arrived for my appointment. That's when the receptionist casually mentioned that I was sitting in the lobby talking with my grandmother and sister. Well, I guess that meeting was not meant to happen, because the next thing I knew, social workers were swooping in from every direction. They hustled me into one room and took my grandmother to another. Obviously, someone had made a big mistake because my grandmother and I were not supposed to be at the agency at the same time. They rushed me into a special session with Dr. Lewis to help me "process" the experience.

She asked if I wanted to get to know my grandmother and sister.

"Of course," I replied.

"Okay, we'll see if we can arrange that," Dr. Lewis said.

Of course, I had a million questions, one of which would define the rest of my life.

"Where is my mother?" I asked. I had not forgotten her. I remembered her smell. I remembered her complexion. I remembered her songbird voice and how she used to sing to me. After all those years, I was still clinging to hope that someday Mom and I would be reunited.

I actually thought that my Mom was crazy and locked up in an institution somewhere. I reasoned that because I was seeing a shrink, I must be crazy and that I probably inherited my craziness from her. But she wasn't institutionalized. That's when Dr. Lewis told me my mother was dead.

Neither one of us made a sound; I just sat there. We both just sat there and looked at each other. Dr. Lewis knew what to expect; I didn't. My heart sank and a tear fell. I turned my head away and looked at the wall, staring at the play I'd written in elementary school and given to Dr. Lewis as a gift. She'd framed it and proudly displayed it all this time. "The Adopted Child" was written when I still had hope of being with my mother again, and now that hope was gone. I would never be able to let her know that I was doing okay and that I would grow up strong and would look after her just as I'd been looking after KB. I would never be able to ask why she never came back.

The only question I could ask Dr. Lewis was "When is the funeral?" At least then, I could say my last good bye.

At that point, Dr. Lewis reached from around her desk and took my hand.

"Shane, your mother died three months ago on December 16. We didn't tell you because it was less than a month after your adoption by the Robertses fell through. We just didn't think you could handle the news at that time; you were going through so much."

"And I'm not now?" I sarcastically jabbed. I was so hurt and angry.

"How could you let them keep that from me? Why didn't somebody tell me that my mother died? I should have been allowed to go to the funeral. No one had the right to withhold that kind of information. I only had one mother, and I should have been able to say good bye."

They'd stolen that moment, and I can never get it back.

I went back to the Balfours that afternoon sobbing bitterly and told my foster mother of three months all the news I had received that day. I was sad, confused, and angry. I desperately needed her to comfort me, hold me, and help make sense of all that happened that day. In a single afternoon, I had met my grandmother, discovered I had a sister, and learned that my mother was dead.

Apparently, Mrs. Balfour decided that a scathing critique of my mother would help me more than the sympathy of a caring parent.

"You have no reason to cry about your mother's death because she never did anything for you anyway," she snapped. "If you all were my children, we would have survived off of bread and water and stayed together as a family."

I could not believe my ears. Her words crushed me and left me not knowing what to feel. All I wanted was to be hugged and made to feel—if only for that moment—that I was not just a foster child. I needed love, compassion, and comforting. Because no one but my own mother had ever held me, not even Mrs. Jenkins, I don't know why I decided to confide in Mrs. Balfour. Why did I set myself up like that? Never again. *Shouldn't I be used to comforting myself by now?*

A few days after meeting my grandmother for the first time, I learned that she had acquired the means to take care of KB and me and to get us out of foster care! She had been offered a larger, subsidized apartment with room enough for her, my sister, KB, and me. Words cannot express the horrible pain and disappointment I felt when I found out that she had refused the offer. I was told that she felt it was just too much, and I was left to wonder why. What was wrong with me? Maybe if I were just a little better behaved, just a little cuter, just a little smarter, maybe then she would want me. Maybe somebody would want me to be his or her kid.

It became painfully clear that during all the time I had been separated from them, my family could have found me. They just didn't want to. Even with the offer of additional housing and resources, my Grandma did not want me. She could have taken the larger apartment, I thought, but she sent us back just like everyone else did. She could have at least tried it out for a while.

One day, about a year or so later, Grandma introduced me to a soft-spoken man with bright eyes. He was her dad. *Wow, this was my great-grandfather.* I couldn't believe I had a great-grandfather. All of my foster parents were in their forties or older. I did not know that great-grandfathers really existed. What was most special about meeting him was something he said to me. He didn't just give me the standard "I'm so happy to see you; I remember when you were in diapers" line. I'd heard it enough times from the family members and friends Grandma introduced me to, and I quickly learned it had little or no meaning. They remembered me when I was in diapers because that's all they could remember.

However, Granddad said, "Shane, I always thought about you. I hoped I'd live to see this day. Here." And he pulled out a white, wrinkled little baby shoe with my name and birthday written in faded blue ink on the side, "I made your mother give me one of your first baby shoes because I knew there was something special about you. See, you were born the night before President Kennedy was killed. The only baby born at that time at your hospital up there in the Bronx."

"Wow, you remember that, Granddad?" I excitedly responded.

"It was late at night, and your mother almost died giving birth to you. In fact, she received her last rites. She was only fifteen years old. They said she wasn't going to make it, but she did. She made it, and you made it, but we lost a President the next afternoon. Don't you ever forget, now, that she also went to the Quonset Hut with your grandmother to have an abortion when they first found out she was pregnant with you. I'm not trying to start nothing, but your grandmother wanted her to finish her schooling. But somebody bigger than you and I had another plan. While lying on the table as they were getting ready to start the procedure, she jumped up suddenly and flew out of there."

He put his hand on my shoulder, looked me in the eye, and said "I didn't know then—and I don't know now—what you're destined to be, but I do know this, son, your life is destined for greatness."

"I have been saving this shoe for you all these years. Your mother would want you to have it now that you and I have been reunited. Because all your baby pictures got lost in that awful fire several years ago, hold on to this shoe. It will keep you close to your mother, and will remind you where you came from and how great the struggle was to get you here."

"Thanks, Granddad. I will hold on to this forever," I said as chills raced up my spine.

Never could I have imagined a moment with my family so genuine and so tender. A humble man who had little material wealth, he gave me what I had been missing in my foster care relationships: a belief in my potential. He let me know that I was valued, that I mattered.

Later in our relationship, Granddad told me that I shouldn't try to solve all my relatives' problems, but I should get on with my own life. I couldn't hear what he was trying to say then, but I hear it now. Granddad thought there was a reason that I was removed from the family. He thought that if I had stayed, I would never have learned the skills I needed to be the man I was supposed to be, and that my life—just as I had lived it—was the perfect way to fulfill my destiny. When Granddad used the word greatness, he didn't mean that everything would be easy for me and that I was a star from the day I was born, but that a transformation and redemption would emerge from the circumstances of my life. To Granddad, greatness was what you did with what God gave you, trusting that God gave it to you for His glory.

Great-granddad's appreciation for me didn't appear to be shared by my grandmother. She agreed to let KB and me come for occasional visits, but the visitations did not last long. On one of my visits, my uncle's ring came up missing. Grandma was told that I had a history of stealing, and she immediately accused me of taking it. I couldn't believe it. I would never ruin my chance to have a relationship with my family by stealing from one of them. No matter how vehemently I insisted that I had not stolen the ring, Grandma wasn't hearing it, and she forbade KB and me to come back to her house after that. A year later, she informed me that my uncle had misplaced the ring somewhere in the house and that it had shown up a few days after she'd thrown us out. She could have told me sooner, or at least made an effort to apologize, but she didn't. At least my name had been cleared.

That was enough for me, but it wasn't nearly enough for KB. He was furious with Grandma for rejecting us again. He could not bring himself to tolerate a grandmother who would turn her back on her grandchildren. I tried to convince him to let it go, but he refused. Motivated by the desire to have a relationship with my sister, I was willing to put up with whatever I had to and to forgive whomever I needed to. I told myself I didn't care how she felt right now. I wanted to tell her that, like the line in the Jennifer Holiday tune *"I'm Not Going":* sooner or later *"you're gonna love me."* I might not get the type of love I need when I need it, but I was determined to show all of them—through the strength of my character—that I was not only worthy of their love, but that I was capable of giving love in return. I have kept working at and chasing this love most of my life.

Learning of my mother's death and being rejected by my grandmother made me lonely, angry, and sad for a while. I started having nightmares and became increasingly bitter toward my little brother. One night while he was asleep, I caught a roach and put it in his ear. It didn't go inside, it just crawled around the outer part, but boy, was it funny watching him jump out of bed screaming.

When adults weren't looking, I would slap or pinch him for no reason. I started resenting him and feeling that he was extra baggage. I was tired of looking after him. Looking after me was enough. I guess brown stuff rolls downhill, and he was the only one I could take it out on. That is an unfair price to pay for being a little brother, and I am sorry for my behavior toward him.

My life was spinning out of control, and I was so unhappy. I started having bouts of wrenching, burning stomach pain from all the stress. Sometimes I'd be in such agony that I would lie in bed and bite my pillow hard enough to tear the pillowcase. I told my foster mom (that twisted wig woman with the crooked glasses), but she didn't believe me. My brother would watch my suffering, and he would cry. As mean as I had been to him at times, he still cared about me. One night he just couldn't stand it anymore, and he bolted out of the bedroom and went to Mrs. Balfour to tell her how much pain I was in. She simply dismissed him.

"There's nothing wrong with Shane; go back to your room," she said. Once again, I got no sympathy from Mrs. Balfour.

On several occasions, I told my social worker, Mr. Pointer, about my stomach pains. He finally insisted that Mrs. Balfour have me evaluated by a doctor, and the doctor discovered that I was developing an ulcer. I took great pleasure in saying, "I told you so," to my foster mother, but she still refused to show any sympathy for me. Instead, she was just downright mean.

"Boy, go to your room. We all have pain. My knees have been hurting me forever, and I've learned to live with it."

I hated her, and I hated living in that house! I never had enough to eat because Mrs. Balfour rationed our food. Fortunately, we were allowed to eat as much bread as we wanted, so I made toast all the time. When I put the bread in, the heat would make the roaches scatter from inside the toaster. It seems disgusting to me now, but I used to get such a kick out of watching the roaches scurry away. I ate so much toast in that house that now—as anyone who knows me will tell you—I do not eat bread unless I am absolutely starving and there is nothing else in driving or walking distance.

I grew sadder with each passing day. Nothing seemed to be going right. I stopped smiling altogether because I simply had nothing to smile about, and I became increasingly evil and rebellious. On several occasions, I slept on the subway riding from one end of the line to the other, well into the night, to avoid going home. Returning one night from an all-day subway ride, I knocked on the door and Mrs. Balfour let me in. I could tell that she had something hidden behind her, but I didn't know what. The next thing I knew, she had hit me over the head with a big metal stirring spoon.

"What did you do that for?" I yelled, but she didn't answer. That really hurt and I was pissed!

I couldn't wait to find some kind of way to get out of that house. I did everything in my power to spend as little time as possible there. I continually came in after curfew just to keep from being at home.

I was fourteen years old, deeply sad, extremely angry, and constantly getting into trouble. While playing outside one day, I was accosted by a neighborhood gang and forced to smoke my first cigarette. They told me that if I didn't try it, they were going to rub my face in the cement.

On another day, I found KB downstairs in front of our apartment building surrounded by a crowd of Latino boys that were about to jump him. I took on three or four of those boys at one time and won. After that, I was in constant danger of being jumped in retaliation, so I had to find a place to lie low for a while. Eventually, I found sanctuary in a dollar movie theater that was down the street that showed Bruce Lee flicks and other old movies. It was not unusual to see strange men in the theater's bathroom masturbating at the urinals. While I was using the bathroom one day, a man standing next to me offered me money if I would leave with him. Oblivious to the danger, I followed him to his car. He unzipped my pants, fondled me, and masturbated. When he was done, he gave me lots of money and drove me back to the theater. I walked to my foster home feeling really confused. Why had I let that happen to me? I really needed someone to help me make sense of it, but I certainly wasn't going to talk to Mrs. Balfour about it.

I eventually started making friends in the Balfour' building. Having friends helped me handle living in the house a little better. Two of my best friends were Robert and his sister, Daphine. They were foster kids like me. Their apartment had carpet and furniture with plastic slipcovers just like the Jenkinses had. Their foster mother, Mrs. Barksdale, was the sweetest woman in the world. I was jealous. *Man, why didn't I get a foster home like this one?* Every time I went upstairs to their apartment, I asked Mrs. Barksdale if there was any way KB and I could live with them. Besides having a much nicer home and decent parents, I liked the idea of living under the same roof with Daphine. I was very attracted to her, and before long she was my girlfriend. Daphine, Robert, and I played upstairs in their room and had lots of fun as often as we could. For me, the Barksdale house was a safe refuge, a home away from hell.

Robert and Daphine's foster parents had a cousin named Joseph. He was in his early twenties, recently discharged from the Marines, and on a fast track as an executive at the telephone company. Joe often came by the house to see Daphine and Robert's older foster brother and sister, the Barksdales' birth children. The Barksdales told Joe about how badly the Balfours were treating me and how unhappy I was. He took an interest in me and took it upon himself to be a big brother to me. Joe spent a lot of time coaching me through my problems and encouraging me to be strong. Sometimes that "be strong" stuff made me mad. *How I can be strong*, I would think to myself. *I have no one.*

Joe helped me realize that there were no other options and that I had no other choice. He had no tolerance for whining. He reminded me frequently that I was smart and that my only chance to change the direction of my life was through education.

"You have to finish school," Joe always said. "That's what matters most."

I knew what Joe was saying was true, but it wasn't that simple. I had so much on my mind all the time. It was just too hard to concentrate in school. How was I supposed to concentrate on schoolwork when I was hopeless, hungry, and homeless? For me, school was just another place where I didn't fit in and where no one seemed to understand me. Most of the time, I fantasized during classes about a life much better than the one I was living, a life where I was actually loved and encouraged to be myself. I was getting so tired of putting on an act in order to fit in; but strangely enough, I was getting good at it.

Joseph drove a sharp, late-model, navy blue Chrysler; he had a nice apartment, and had many well-established friends. Hanging around him exposed me to successful people and a standard of living I had not seen before. His friends became my role models. I wanted to be just like them. I got along much better with them than I did with people my age. Joe was also a great father to his little girl, and I really admired that.

Eventually, the things Joe said started sinking in. I started thinking, *if I want nice things like he has, maybe I should take his advice.*

My "big brother," Joe made me feel as if I mattered. He always kept his word and showed up when he promised. I looked up to him. At a time when my life could have gone in any direction, his interest in me was like a bridge over troubled water. More important, he taught me that the best way to cross over troubled water is to count on no one other than self and to develop the tools necessary to build your own bridges. He kept drilling it into my head that I would always be at the mercy of others if I did not have my own tools. By "tools," he meant education, communication skills, and experience. What he said was true, but I later learned that you do need to know how to depend on people every now and then during times of trouble. You just have to hope they've really got your back and will show up when you need them.

◆   ◆   ◆

It was a cold and very sad day when the news broke that Mrs. Barksdale had had a sudden heart attack and died. Stunned, I ran upstairs to find Daphine and Robert. As we hugged each other, Robert said, "I don't know what's going to happen to us now."

I started to cry, and all I could say was, "It'll be all right."

The morning of the funeral seemed like a bad dream. The limousine and hearse were parked outside the building. Joe and the funeral directors led us downstairs for the procession to the church. I remember Joe whispering to me, "Keep it together. Don't go making any performance."

"What did he mean by that?" I remember thinking. Was I not supposed to cry? Why was I always being told to mask my emotions?

A few days later, Daphine and Robert were moved to another foster home, and I never saw them again.

It wasn't too long afterward that, during a routine visit, Mr. Pointer asked KB and me if we were ready to move out of Mrs. Balfour's house. In unison and without a moment of hesitation, we both said, "Yes."

"How does living in a group home sound?" he asked.

Everything I knew about life in a group home I had learned from watching "Fish," a popular television sitcom at the time. The kids on the show seemed to have lots of fun, so we agreed. There was, however, one condition—KB and I would be separated. They couldn't send siblings to the same group home. Surprisingly, the thought of being separated was not a big deal to either of us. We were getting tired of each other anyway, or so we thought. With all the years of brotherly fights and sharing rooms, we thought it would be good not to be around each other for a while. I knew I was tired of having him around. Carrying him was a heavy burden. I needed to be free for a while from the responsibility of looking after the two of us. I needed time to look out for myself and be on my own.

4

Someday

Keep on walking tall,
hold your head up high,
lay your dreams up to the sky,
sing your greatest song,
and you'll keep going on
take it from me; someday we'll
all be free....

—A. Keyes

My little brother KB and I moved into separate group homes. I moved into a large group home on Lacombe Avenue in the Soundview section of the Bronx. Mr. and Mrs. Hopkins, the house parents, lived in an apartment upstairs during the week and drove to their house in Connecticut on weekends. The kitchen refrigerators had steel doors that were locked unless meals were being prepared. The home had a diverse mix of children, including some in wheelchairs, which was hard to get used to at first. However, I quickly realized that we all had a lot in common. They had the same hopes and fears that I did. They wanted to be happy, just as I did. They were misunderstood, just as I had been. And, just like me, someone had rejected them.

I'll always remember Eric. A resident of the home, he had been born with no arms or legs. I made the mistake once of mouthing off to him. I thought, if there's anyone I should be able to mouth off to and get away with it, it would be the kid with no arms and legs. Eric taught me a lesson or two. That dude hopped out of his wheelchair onto the floor faster than a speeding bullet. He picked me up with one of his upper stubs, threw me to the floor, and whipped my butt with the other stub. I didn't know what hit me, literally. He quickly earned my respect. I had to learn what everyone in the house already knew: *don't mess with Eric*. There was more strength in those short stubs than most of us have in our arms.

Another person who taught me something was Eugene. He was also in a wheelchair. We became very close friends. Eugene, who had cerebral palsy, was one of the smartest and most compassionate people I had ever met. He was like a brother to me.

In fact, there was a bond among all the kids in the house that transcended ethnicity or disability. This home was different from any I had ever lived in.

There was one thing, unfortunately, that being in a new home had not changed: I still found a way to get into a tremendous amount of trouble. Some of the guys and I would take Eric on the train in his wheelchair. Grasping a can between his stubs, he would beg passengers for money. At the end of the day, we would equally split everything we collected, and, boy, would we clean up!

It was also the time in my life when I started experimenting with weed, beer, and cigarettes. Hanging out with the boys one night, I put down a quart of Olde English, smoked a joint, and had my first Salem cigarette. My head was spinning so badly and my stomach was so upset that I thought I was going to die. When I came back to the group home, I tried to lie down but the room kept spinning. I promised myself that if I lived through the night, I would never do that again. When I woke up the next morning, I found myself on restriction—a group home term for punishment—for two weeks. I regret that it did not deter me. My desire to fit in with the boys was much greater than my fear of being punished. I just figured I would smoke and drink a little less the next time around.

During my stay at the Soundview Group Home, I developed grand mal epileptic seizures. I couldn't believe it. I'd already been through hell in my short, fourteen-year life. Now my body was under attack by those seizures, which seemed to come upon me without warning and for no apparent reason. I was angry and depressed. The last thing I wanted was another challenge in my life, and here I was with epilepsy—something else to make me feel like a freak. The doctors put me on Dilantin and Phenobarbital to bring the seizures under control, but the drugs didn't work and the seizures continued until my junior year of high school. Then, just as abruptly as they had started, they went away. While they lasted, I ignored them as much as I could and went on with my life.

It was at Soundview that I met one of my best female friends ever. Vanessa was kind and loving, but also no-nonsense. She was just as tough as she was kind and would kick your butt in a minute. We never dated or anything, but Vanessa and I developed an extremely close friendship. Vanessa introduced me to her parents, Mr. and Mrs. Moragne. I grew to like them so much, and Vanessa and I were so close, that I asked Vanessa if I could live with her family. I was so disappointed when they said I couldn't, but we all remained very close, and Vanessa and I started referring to each other as brother and sister.

I had been attending the New York School of Printing High School for about a year when I auditioned for the theater program at Julia Richman High School for the Performing Arts. I was determined to fulfill my dream of becoming an actor so I could show all those people who did not want me that I was special. I knew I had a gift for acting and that it might just be a way out of my seemingly inescapable loneliness and rejection.

I jumped, screamed, and ran up and down the stairs the day I got my acceptance letter to Julia Richman. There was no doubt in my mind that I was destined to be a great movie star. Becoming a student at this highly regarded school was the first step toward fulfilling that dream. Every day was a great day at Julia Richman. I worked hard in my acting classes, determined to perfect my craft. One of the most exciting moments from that period of my life was when MGM studios held auditions at our school for the movie "Fame." I auditioned for the part of Leroy, and I must have really impressed MGM because I got a callback. However, I guess it just was not my time because the part of Leroy went to one of my school rivals, Gene Anthony Ray. Gene was an awesome dancer with a nasty attitude, but, in my opinion, could not act. Because of this view, I thought for sure I was going to get the part, but I guess they wanted a dancer, not an actor.

At the movie's premier, I was sick with envy. I could not help but wonder what my life might be like if I were up on that movie screen playing Leroy instead of Gene. "Fame" had taken Gene out of the hood to the kind of life I wanted so badly. For me, it was back to the hood and living in the group home. It was not very long after that, though, that I got a different kind of ticket out of the hood. The social workers had identified another adoptive family for me. It would be in Rochester, New York, with an unmarried Baptist minister.

♦   ♦   ♦

Reverend Kennedy had already successfully adopted a six-year-old boy. That record of accomplishment gave me hope that perhaps this time an adoption would finally work for KB and me. However, KB wanted no part of family living again. The thought of being with a family again and being rejected was just too painful. The Jenkinses had let him down, and the Robertses had tossed us aside after two months. He decided that group-home living, without any emotional attachments, was safer, but I saw this as a chance for us to be reunited and a chance for me to take care of him the way I used too. I knew he needed me.

While we were separated, KB's behavior had been getting bad. He started stealing bicycles and getting into all kinds of trouble. No one could get through to him. The social workers kept asking me to talk to KB about his behavior because I was the only one he would listen to. That's why I didn't want to pass up the chance for this adoption. I didn't even care that Rochester was so far away from New York City; maybe that was a good thing. It seemed that I had experienced nothing but pain in the Big Apple anyway, so I took charge of the situation and told KB that we were going to do this—whether he wanted to or not. It was a chance for us to be loved, happy, and secure. Besides, we had started to miss our living with each other, and deep down I knew he wanted to be with his big brother. He must have known that I would find a way for us to be together again, and this was it.

In my mind, being adopted and having a family was the absolute answer to all of my troubles. I dreamed constantly of living in a big house, having a nice car, and wearing nice clothes. It hurt so much whenever I would hear other children talk about their parents. It did not matter whether what they said about them was good or bad, at least they had parents. I wanted my own mom and dad. Besides, it was my job to protect KB. A family meant security, and if anything ever happened to me, he would be safe.

I realized that the clock was running out for us because we were no longer two cuddly little boys in need of a home. We were teenagers now, and people were not knocking down doors to take in kids like us. On the day we met with Reverend Kennedy for the first time, I whispered to KB, "Look, man, don't blow it. Smile a lot. We have to be on our best behavior."

It worked! After a few visits, we were leaving the past behind and moving out of New York City to Rochester. I had another chance at my lifelong dream of having a family we could call our own.

Once again, we were starting fresh with a new home and a new dad. I decided that I wanted to mark the new beginning by changing my name. Somehow, I reasoned that the name Shane had brought me and everyone else around me only heartache. My new dad's only stipulation was that I had to research the meaning of my new name and write a full page explaining why I chose it. I picked the name Karim, which means "generous." My full name became Karim Abdu Jamar Kennedy. KB just decided to change his middle name from Earl to Elliott.

At our new home, I was excited to have a new little brother who had also been adopted. His name was Marcus, and we hit it off immediately. I think KB was a little jealous of him. At the same time KB seemed happy to finally be a big brother and that he would attend the same school as Marcus: St. Louis Catholic School in Pittsford, New York. My new dad took me on site visits to choose a school. We visited two public high schools, one all-boys Catholic school, and one co-ed Catholic school. After touring and meeting with principals of all four schools, he asked me to rate them in my order of preference. I thought it was so cool that he was going to let me choose. Eager to exercise this wonderful new freedom, I quickly rated the two public high schools one and two, the Catholic co-ed school number three, and the all-boys Catholic school last. I turned my preferences over to Dad, who looked at them and said, "You will be attending St. Thomas Aquinas."

It was the most academically rigorous of the four and the one with no girls. I wanted to know why he had bothered to ask my opinion, only to select the one I chose as my last preference. He said that St. Thomas Aquinas would be the most challenging, and he thought black boys needed academic challenges to prepare them for manhood. Then my dad hit me with the biggie. He told me that I would start this new school in the ninth grade, although New York City Public Schools (NYCPS) had duly promoted me to the tenth grade. He said he had no confidence in the NYCPS curriculum because the standards were inferior. Okay, I admit my grades sucked, but I *was* passing, even though it was with C's and D's.

My attitude toward Reverend Kennedy changed. Why did this big, fat, Afro-wearing dude think he could come into my life and tell my school to make me repeat a grade? As if that was not bad enough, I had to cut off my long-awaited mustache because the school did not allow boys to have facial hair. From that moment on, I was convinced he was a bona fide butt-hole, and group home living looked like paradise. At least there I was able to make my own decisions.

There was no changing my dad's mind about how things were going to be. I was enrolled at predominantly white St. Thomas Aquinas. I made friends quickly, especially with the few black kids that were there. All of them came from very good homes with strong values. They followed the rules, did their homework on time, and stayed out of trouble.

One kid stood out from the others. He appeared unhappy and angry and acted as if he did not want to be there. He was the notorious school "bad boy," so naturally I wanted to be friends with him. I was actually afraid of him until we discovered that we had a lot in common. Neither of us was living with our parents, and Kevin's parents were struggling with substance abuse the way my mother had. Kevin and I were drawn to each other and hit it off right from the start. Meeting him was like a ray of sunshine coming through prison bars.

I had started to feel like a prisoner living with my new dad. He actually screened my letters from my grandmother, my friend Vanessa, her parents, and other folks from New York City. He forbade me to remain in contact with my family and New York friends, saying it was out of concern for the kind of influence they might have over me while I was adjusting to my new home. I didn't understand his rationale. I was mad and felt cut off from the world I'd known all of my life. The more he tried to make me forget my past, the more I longed to hold on to it.

With Dad's permission, I decided to join the school band.

"What instrument do you want to play?" Dad asked.

"The teacher said he has space only in the percussion section, so I can play either the drums or the xylophone."

"I didn't ask you what the band instructor said. I asked *you* what instrument *you* want to play."

"I've always wanted to play the trombone."

"Then that's what you'll play." he declared.

As he drove me to the music shop that night, I wondered how I was going to just show up at school with a trombone, when the teacher had said there was room only in the percussion section.

The next day, Dad went to school with me and spoke privately with the band teacher. I don't know what he said, but I played the trombone in the band that year. Now that was cool. I had never had anyone go to bat for me like that before. "Is this what it means to be somebody's kid?" I wondered. "Is this what real parents do for their children?" All I knew for sure was that, at that moment, I felt special.

On another occasion, the school sent a note home that said I had to shave off my little peach fuzz of a mustache. Once again my dad stood up for me, and I became one of the only kids in school who didn't have to shave. In my eyes, Dad had more than redeemed himself. I was once again beginning to dig this family thing.

Meanwhile, KB and I worked at living with each other once more. We started having fights over the pettiest things. One Sunday after church, I flew into a rage over socks. I noticed that my white tube socks were damaged beyond repair.

No matter how many times I tell KB not to wear my clothes he never listens, I fumed. *Dad doesn't do anything to KB when he does something wrong, so KB just does whatever he wants.*

After a few minutes of egging myself on, I was furious, and before I knew it, I was screaming at the top of my lungs, "I'm so sick of this shit"!

I'm not sure if it was the fact that I cursed, or the fact that I cursed on a Sunday, but my dad must have been on his way to the kitchen before the words were out of my mouth. He came flying into the room and slapped me upside my head. Shocked, angry, and extremely embarrassed, I ran upstairs and locked myself in my room. I lay across the bed for what seemed like hours, growing more distraught about my life with every minute. *This adoption is going down the tubes fast*, I decided. *They always like KB better than me*. I reached the conclusion that I couldn't do anything right.

I decided that the best course of action was to kill myself. I looked at my Dilantin, and without hesitation swallowed all of the pills. As I sat on my bed, my eyes got heavy, and I became extremely groggy. Convinced that I was on my way to certain death, I reconsidered and stumbled downstairs to tell Dad what I had done. He hustled KB, Marcus, and me into the car and rushed to the hospital. The emergency-room physician chastised me for trying to take my life.

"Nothing could be that bad," he said. "Oh, yes, it could" I mumbled under my breath. "Living with my dad is hell."

As they were getting the pills out of my system, I overheard Dad say to the doctors and nurses that he wanted this to be a miserable and unforgettable experience for me. Against medical advice, he signed me out of the hospital. On the way home, he stopped at a steak house and parked the car near the kitchen where I could fully experience the nauseating aroma of food cooking.

The next morning, despite being at the hospital extremely late, Dad woke me up bright and early for school. When we arrived at school, he walked me into the principal's office and issued clear instructions to the faculty that I was to attend all classes regardless of how I felt. Although the school usually respected his wishes, when they learned what I'd been through the night before, they let me go to the guidance counselor's office, where I slept most of the day. I felt vindicated. Even the school felt Dad was being unreasonable. In my mind, the same father who had made me feel special by standing up for me had now turned completely against me. *Okay, I get the message* I thought. *Maybe attempting to kill myself is something I'll think twice about next time; but if this mental anguish keeps up, I'll finish what I started.*

My dad's unconventional perspective started making me unpopular at school. After a few weeks of checking my homework, he decided that I wasn't bringing home a sufficient amount. "Oh, this won't work," he said. "I'll have to let them know that I'm paying too much tuition for them to be sending this nonsense home and calling it homework."

And that's exactly what he did. As a result, the homework load for the entire class doubled, and somehow it got out that this was as a direct result of my dad's actions. I caught much grief from the entire class including, my boy Kevin.

When Dad found out that I was friends with "bad boy" Kevin, he told me not to associate with him during school so I could focus fully on my academic priorities. Kevin and I started talking on the phone late into the night to compensate for the fact that we couldn't talk at school anymore. One night we talked until 2:00 a.m. about everything from sex to drugs, not knowing that my dad was eavesdropping.

The next morning all hell broke loose. Dad jumped all over me and forbade me to have any contact with Kevin ever again. He even asked Kevin's grandmother to help him enforce his new rule, but, fortunately, she ignored him and continued to let me hang out with Kevin at her place. With each day that passed, I was growing more and more resentful of Dad. If this was what having a father meant, then maybe I didn't need one.

When the nearby all-girls school partnered with our all-boys school to have a dance, Dad insisted on meeting my date beforehand. Before I could call someone a friend, he had to approve. The night of the dance, my date's parents dropped her off at my house where I introduced her to Dad. Well, she seemed to pass inspection because he allowed us to leave for the dance without any objections. After I got home from a fantastic evening, Dad said that he disapproved of my date because she didn't stand up to greet him. *How ridiculous*, I thought; living with this man was just getting to be too much.

My resentment toward my dad continued to grow. I started complaining about him to anyone who'd listen. Even the adults I confided in agreed that he was simply too unreasonable.

Finally, I decided it was time to get away from Reverend Kennedy for good. I ran away to Kevin's house with no intention of ever returning. Regrettably, that was the first place Dad looked for me, and he had me back home in a matter of a few hours. I ran away several more times after that, and each time Dad would call the same big black police officer to fetch me home.

Determined to finally run away and not be caught, I saved enough money to get a bus ticket back to New York City. I had several hours before my bus was scheduled to leave, so I called Dad's mother, Grandma Kennedy. She asked me where I was, but I wouldn't tell her, fearing she'd blab to Dad. She told me that she felt bad about how unreasonable my father was being and implied that she understood what I was going through. My defenses were lowered by her empathy and somehow I really did think I could trust her. I told her where I was, and she offered to take me to her place to get some sleep before I got on the bus the next morning. On the way to her house, Grandma stopped by Dad's house "just to get your pajamas," she promised.

She had me duck down in the back seat so Dad couldn't see me. She retrieved the pajamas, and we were on our way. About thirty minutes after arriving at Grandma's, the doorbell rang. To my surprise, it was Dad and the same police officer who had chased me down so many times before.

"Shane, do you think I have nothing better to do but chase you around Rochester?" the officer quipped.

"As long as you keep sending me back to his house, you are going to have to keep chasing me," I shot back.

I didn't know then that I would never go back there.

They took me to a place called Hillside Children's Center. It was a cold place with heavy metal doors that locked tight behind me as I entered the building. They told me that I would be staying at

Hillside for two weeks and that Dad was forbidden to see me while counselors helped me work out my problems. At the end of the two weeks, a Rochester social worker and my social worker from New York City, Mr. Pointer, met with my dad and me. They asked if I wanted to go back to Dad's house. I quickly responded with a firm, "No!" They said that Dad wanted me home and was willing to change some of his parenting techniques.

Yeah, he might change, but I doubt it, I thought. I didn't want to take that chance. I told them that there was no way I would ever go back. I looked up and was shocked to see a tear fall from my dad's eye. Seeing him cry for the first time made me think about staying with him, but I couldn't give in. I just couldn't. In fact, a part of me wanted to cause him as much pain as I could.

I looked him straight in the eye and spoke words that I hoped would hurt him as all my parents before him had hurt me.

"I'm 15, and you're 25. What makes you think you can ever be my father?" Everyone stared at me in disbelief. I just stared right back, determined not to display any trace of sadness.

"Reverend Kennedy is willing to keep your brother KB whether

you stay or not, someone said.

"If KB has a chance to have a family, that's great. No problem. I am not going to stand in the way," I responded. Besides, KB was not having the same problems I was. He was a good kid. Then Dad said something that truly pierced my heart.

"If you leave, there's no coming back. And you can never see or talk to KB again."

Swallowing an orange-sized lump in my throat, I looked at him and everyone else in the room and said, "If that's what it takes, no problem."

Tears fell down my face as the magnitude of my decision sank in. I had agreed to leave my brother behind, which meant leaving my heart and a piece of my soul behind. Without KB, what was my purpose for living? My biggest accomplishment so far was being his parent. It was my life task. He was safe. He had a family. Perhaps I was a bad influence on him. Maybe KB would be better off without me. I needed to focus on getting my life straight now. At that moment, I accepted the reality that my dream of having a family would never materialize.

It made me sad, but I knew it was true. It was time to go. I declared that there would be no more trying to hit targets that kept moving. No more trying to be cute enough to win over families or behaving well enough not to be kicked out of one. I realized some dreams just could not be. From that moment on, I knew I was all that I had, and I was determined to survive.

My eyes were red and swollen from crying by now, but Mr. Pointer knew my mind was made up.

"Well, Shane, how do you want to travel back to New York City?"

"I've never been on a plane before," I confessed, my voice quivering.

Doing his best to console me and lift my spirits, he said, "Then let's fly back, Shane." And we did.

Once again, Mr. Pointer was there to help me pick up the broken pieces of my life. He was more than a social worker to me; he was like family. It was obvious from day one that he really cared about me. For some odd reason, he thought I had potential. He really believed in me and believed me. When I was sad, he would be standing to the side, fighting back tears, but he was also a tough, no-nonsense guy. I never quite figured out how to manipulate him. Mr. Pointer gave me only so much rope before yanking it back.

The flight from Rochester to New York City was my first airplane ride, and it was very exciting; but it was sad that Mr. Pointer didn't have a place for me to stay when I returned to New York City. He asked me if I had any ideas.

"How about the Moragnes?" I suggested.

"Why don't you call them and see if they would be willing to be an emergency foster home for you?"

I called Vanessa and she asked her parents, who promptly agreed to take me in for a while. They had never liked Reverend Kennedy anyway.

5

A Dream With Your Name On It

Stand tall, don't you be afraid,
you're sure to find your way
when that voice that's deep inside you
says to take a chance—
that's what you have to do.
Follow your heart—
go where it leads you.
It's telling you—
there's a dream out there with your name
on it.

—J. Holiday

Back in New York City, I was determined to make the most of my life. I had two failed adoptive placements under my belt, and there was something I wanted to prove to myself and to all those who repeatedly said I'd never amount to anything. Fortunately, the Moragne's were willing to give me a place to stay while Mr. Pointer and I sorted things out. The Moragne's lived in Mitchell Houses, one of the better public housing developments. I didn't smell urine in the elevators as much as I had in some of the others, and it wasn't roach infested.

My return to New York was emotionally difficult. I had just been separated from my brother again and had to accept that I would likely never again see or speak to him. My seizures started coming with greater frequency and intensity. I was in and out of the hospital all the time. At one point, the seizures were occurring so often that the neurologist expressed serious concern about their effect on my nervous system. It was obvious what was happening. I was grieving for my brother and the lost relationship with a father as if they had both died. I would not have made it through all that without Pop Moragne. He and I really connected, and his presence had a comforting and calming influence on me.

While the social workers were completing the paperwork so the Moragnes could become my long-term foster parents, doctors discovered that Mom Moragne had been exposed to TB. That meant I had to be immediately removed from their home. Thanks to a positive TB test, I was going to have to leave a place where I finally felt comfortable and had been accepted unconditionally.

"This can't be happening," I groaned. I was beginning to think I shouldn't bother to unpack. Whenever I moved someplace new, I was never there long. I hated having to leave the Moragnes, but I had no choice.

Mr. Pointer was able to find yet another foster family for me, this time in the Bushwick section of Brooklyn. Mr. and Mrs. Edwards had a son and a daughter. They also had a teenage foster child named Fritz living with them. It was clear from the very beginning that they planned to adopt Fritz and that they had no interest in adopting me. What foster parent wouldn't have wanted to adopt Fritz? He was easygoing, didn't tall back, and helped around the house. The closest thing he had to a vice was an occasional basketball game. I, unfortunately, was nothing like Fritz.

Mr. and Mrs. Edwards were devout Roman Catholics. The house was filled with statues of Mary, Jesus, and Joseph. There was a strong Muslim community in the neighborhood as well. Although I was growing up under the supervision of a Catholic agency and I'd had strong Catholic influences from the Jenkins family, I had always been impressed and intrigued by Muslims. They were so neatly dressed and seemed so disciplined. I started thinking that maybe self-discipline was what was missing in my life. Maybe, if I were more disciplined, I could focus better in school. Maybe if I focused in school, I would achieve my goals—just as my big brother Joe had always said I should. I started paying a lot more attention to the Muslims—the way the women revealed only their eyes and the men draped themselves in clothing from head to toe. When a man's head was exposed, he always had a very neat, close-tapered haircut. To me, they stood out and represented themselves well.

On my way home one day, I stopped into the neighborhood mosque, talked with some of the brothers there, and decided to have my Shahada (the equivalent of Christian baptism). I selected a Muslim name (Elijah Abdullah Kareem Abdula Muhammad [EAKAM for short]). I told the brothers of the Ansar Allah Community that I was homeless. I had a place to sleep with a foster family, but it wasn't really home for me. I told them that the Catholic Home Bureau was my guardian and that none of the homes they had found for me had worked out. I asked the brothers if they would adopt me and let me grow up as a Muslim. The brothers welcomed me. They said they were willing to adopt me and that they would be happy to have my social worker visit their community to determine if it was a suitable place for me to live. They even said they would send me to college if my grades were good enough, but they would decide my field of study based on the needs of their community. That probably meant my career in theater was out of the question. However, for what I'd get in return—safety, security, discipline, and a permanent home—I thought it was a good tradeoff. Besides, I had felt drawn to the Muslims for quite some time. I was sure that this was the right place for me.

I returned to Mrs. Edwards that day dressed as a new Muslim, wearing all white and feeling euphoric. When Mrs. Edwards opened the door, she looked as if she had seen a ghost. She pulled herself together long enough to ask, "Did any of the neighbors see you coming down the street?" She seemed quite frazzled. Apparently, the sight of me in Muslim clothing had sent her over the edge. "I can't take any more of this; they're going to have to do something with you. I can't have you around here dressed like that," she complained.

Mrs. Edwards phoned Mr. Pointer and told him that I had to go immediately. I don't know what Mr. Pointer said, but she calmed down and handed me the phone. I told Mr. Pointer that I had asked the Muslims to adopt me and that they said they would. He immediately set up an appointment to visit the mosque.

I don't know what happened during Mr. Pointer's visit to the Ansar Allah Community, but it definitely had an effect on him. He told me that if I ever went back there, I would be sent straight to Juvenile Hall. I supposed he thought that would be the end of it, but I refused to accept his decision. I knew enough to realize that I had the constitutional right to practice the religion of my choice, and I called the New York Legal Aid Society for help. I explained to the woman who answered the phone that I was a foster child under the guardianship of the Catholic Home Bureau, and that I had just become a Muslim.

"Don't I have a constitutional right to freedom of religion?" I demanded to know.

I could not have been more disappointed when she told me that as long as I was a ward of the state, the state was my guardian, and I had to do what they said. I could practice whatever religion I wanted when I turned 18. That's when it hit me that I was the property of New York State, and the state controlled my every move. Whether I wanted to or not, I had to accept Mr. Pointer's decision.

I never went back to the mosque again.

Thankfully, Mrs. Edwards got over being upset that I had become a Muslim and decided to allow me to remain in their home until other arrangements could be made for me. I was happy to have a place to stay, but what I really wanted was to be out of foster care, to be on my own, and to make my own decisions. The decisions other people were making for me just seemed to screw up my life. I was sure I could do better. For now, however, it was back to stay with the Edwards family.

The Bushwick neighborhood wasn't a very safe part of Brooklyn. In retrospect, I probably shouldn't have been riding the subway alone to school and to visits with my social worker. One day while I was returning home after seeing Mr. Pointer, excited about my new eyeglasses that I had bought with money I had earned and saved, a deranged man appeared from nowhere and attacked me. I'd noticed him loudly babbling to himself earlier when I got on the train, but didn't pay him much attention because people are always talking to themselves on the subway. He switched seats several times while the train emptied, until there were less than a handful of people in the car. The next thing I knew, he had cornered me in my seat and was beating me up. It continued for several stops.

A white-haired old woman attempted to intervene on my behalf.

"Bitch, mind your own business, before I kick your ass," he barked.

She retreated to the far end of the train, and he continued to hit me.

The first punch broke my new glasses. All I could do was cover my face and curl up like a baby as this man pounded his fists into my back and head.

As the train pulled into the next station he suddenly stopped beating me, and I ran from the train and found a police officer standing on the platform. When I explained what had happened, he followed me back on the train, handcuffed my attacker, and led us to a back room in the subway station.

With the door shut, the police officer took out his club and beat the living daylights out of the man. After administering several hard blows, he paused and asked me if I had seen anything.

"No," I said, so he continued to pummel the guy. As my attacker screamed in pain, the officer kept calling him a punk for picking on a little kid.

I don't know how long the beating lasted or if it continued after I left; I just wanted to go home. My face was badly bruised and my body was sore.

◆　　　◆　　　◆

While living with the Edwards family, I decided to try to strengthen my relationship with my grandmother. She had rejected me repeatedly, but I was determined not to abandon the relationship. I started visiting her more frequently, and in the process began developing a relationship with my Uncle Johnny. Everyone was afraid of Uncle Johnny because he had served a long sentence in a facility for the criminally insane. He got very excited whenever I visited and would ask me to read the Bible to him. Almost everyone in the family avoided him except me. I liked him. At the time, he and his sister, Cookie, were the only people in the family who made me feel wanted. I later learned from Grandma that Johnny was my mom's favorite brother.

One day I arrived at my grandmother's house to find a tall man visiting her. Grandma introduced him as her old boyfriend, Vernon. She introduced me as Dee Dee's son.

"Dee Dee's son? Who's Dee Dee?" I wondered to myself.

Seeing the puzzled look on my face, Grandma said, "Sit down, Shane." I figured something big was about to be revealed, and I was right. Grandma told me that Vernon was my birth father's brother.

"Your dad's name is David," she continued. "Dee Dee is a nickname." That's when Vernon spoke up.

"This is Shane? Oh my God! I haven't seen you since you were in diapers!"

The news was shocking, but it felt so good to meet someone who remembered me. I was even more delighted to learn that he knew where my father was.

"Would you tell him I'd like to see him," I asked, trying hard to contain my excitement.

"Oh, he wants to see you too."

I couldn't believe it. Someone knew where my father was, and he wanted to see me! It was all I could do not to jump up and down screaming. I asked Uncle Vernon to ask my father to get in touch with me right away.

I left Grandma's that day extremely happy. I had decided to stay in touch with her. This one visit alone had given me more hope than I'd had in years that I would finally find one person in this world who really wanted me.

The next day, the phone rang before daylight, and it was my father.

"Hello, Shane?"

My heart was racing. "Yes. This is Shane."

"Oh my God!" he screamed. "It's my son!"

His excitement was exhilarating. I could feel how genuinely thrilled he was to find me.

"I have thought about you every day. I love you, son. I've always loved you." He said he had tried to find me but that everyone had lied to him about where I was. They'd even lied to him about my name.

"I thought your name was David," he said. "When can I see you?"

"How about today," I answered.

Before I could hang up the phone, my dad was on his way. I couldn't believe it. As a little boy, I fantasized about meeting my father. I imagined that he was rich and that my being in foster care was just a big mistake. I couldn't wait to see what he was really like.

A few hours later, he arrived.

Right away, I realized he wasn't going to live up to my rich father fantasy. He was driving a loud, rusty, beat-up old car. He didn't even bother to park it. He threw open the door and practically leapt out. We ran to meet one another, and he grabbed me and lifted me off the ground. He held me and kept saying over and over again, "My son, my son," and he cried.

"He ain't rich and he ain't tall, I thought. *But he is my father.* That was enough for me. I searched his face looking for the family resemblance. We looked alike. Finally, after all these years, I looked like somebody else. When we finally let go of each other, I noticed a very attractive woman stepping from the passenger side of the car.

"This is Joanne," he said proudly.

I was thinking that my dad had really good taste in women when he asked me if I wanted to ride with them to his apartment. I immediately said, "yes."

We piled into the rickety old car and started out for Dad's place in the Fort Apache section of the Bronx. I was so pumped that on the drive over I couldn't stop talking. I wanted to tell him everything that had ever happened to me. Who knew if we would ever have this chance again? I listened closely to his every word too, hoping to find out as much about him and my family as I could. There was no question he wouldn't answer. We were both so excited. His rusty old car was extremely noisy, so we had to talk loud. That was okay. I was with my father! I could put up with a little noise. However, what I saw when we pulled up to his place really tested my tolerance.

My father lived in a condemned building. Most of the apartments had been vacated, and wires were running from one apartment to the next to share electricity. There were plenty of rats and roaches, but no hot water. The ceiling was caving in, and the walls were filthy. Unbelievably, after a while I didn't care. He was my father, and I wanted to be wherever he was. I told him I was not going back to my foster home and that I wanted to stay with him.

"This is your home, son; you don't have to go back." His words made me so happy that I was speechless. All I could do was hug him and cry.

I moved in with Dad right away, and we started to get better acquainted. I was quite surprised when he told me that I had sixteen brothers and sisters. The woman he married had had three children before she died—David Jr., Adrienne, and Debbie—who were being raised by their maternal grandmother. Another sister lived with relatives in the Caribbean. The rest were in foster care or adopted. He said they knew about me and that he couldn't wait for me to meet them all.

I had been living with my father for just a few days when it was time for my subway assault case to be heard in court. It felt great having Dad go to court with me. He wanted to see who attacked his son. My chest was poked out so far I almost busted my buttons. *My father will kick your butt if you mess with me*, I mouthed to myself as we sat in the courtroom together. I felt protected like never before.

At last I felt safe, and the outcome of the case was good too. The judge ruled that my attacker had to stay away from me for six months, and victim's compensation paid for the glasses he had broken.

Outside the court, my father confronted the man and told him what he'd do to him if he ever saw him again. That small act made my father my hero.

However, just like almost every other good thing in my life, my fantasy of what life would be like with my real family was quickly destroyed. I found out that my father made a living selling stolen toys and bootlegged VHS tapes on the street. He thought I would be a natural at selling things, so he took me with him on several occasions. I never really wanted to go. I wanted him to make an honest living. At the same time, I wanted to be with him and to make an effort to understand his world.

As the days passed, his world kept getting scarier and scarier to me. People came knocking on the door at all hours of the night. I was never allowed to answer, and they were never invited in. Once I peeped into his bedroom and saw him scraping white powder off the folding table beside his bed. I knew enough to know it was cocaine. *Oh, my God, my father has cocaine. Is that why people are knocking at the door all night?* As much as I didn't want it to be true, I now knew that my dad was distributing and selling drugs.

In spite of his unorthodox enterprises, my dad tried to make living with him as safe and normal as possible. He enrolled me in Alfred E. Smith High School. That meant I had to leave my friends at Julia Richman behind. It was hard to leave because my last few months at Julia Richman were turning out to be some of my best.

I was finally able to produce the musical play I had written while living with Reverend Kennedy—"Ebony and the Seven Dudes"— a Black version of "Snow White and the Seven Dwarfs." Rodney, who was a classmate of mine, introduced me to his mom, and she gave me her typewriter so I could type my musical. She told me I could keep it if I promised to take good care of it. I secured backers to finance the costumes and props and found a junior high school that would allow me to use the auditorium. My father had high hopes that my production would take us from rags to riches (and I thought *I* was a big dreamer!), but this was an amateur play performed in a junior high school auditorium. It was great fun, and I'll always remember it, but it wasn't "Dreamgirls."

During that summer, I signed up for a job as a counselor in a children's day camp. I enjoyed the job, but at the end of each day, I was exhausted. The best part of the job was going on field trips. I couldn't believe I was actually being paid to go out and have fun with those kids. On one of our field trips to Jones Beach, a child's beach ball got away. It was already quite a distance from the shore by the time I saw it. Oblivious to any danger, I swam out to retrieve it. Several minutes later, I looked back at the shore, realized how far out in the ocean I was, and panicked. I started swimming as hard as I could, but I tired quickly and started going under. In a few seconds, I had swallowed so much water that I thought I was going to die. A lifeguard saw me and, after a considerable struggle, managed to pull me safely to shore. Needless to say, I didn't come back with the beach ball, but I did come back with my life. I was so embarrassed that I wanted to quit that job, but with the encouragement of my supervisor and several coworkers, I managed to hang in there and finish the summer.

My father knew I'd made some extra money at the camp, and he wasn't shy about asking me for it. In fact, he started asking me for money with greater and greater frequency. At first I didn't mind, but after a while I noticed that none of it was going to buy groceries. I made the mistake of sharing my frustration with my father's Uncle Erby.

Uncle Erby drank a fifth of Scotch every day, but he had a nice car, a nice apartment, and a doting wife, so everybody respected him. I told him that I was the only one in the house working a legitimate job. Uncle Erby said he would talk to Dad. After talking with my father, Uncle Erby reported to me that Dad was *really* pissed. He told Uncle Erby that I was a liar, but Uncle Erby believed me. He gave me money to buy my own food and invited me to church with him that next Sunday. He suggested that I get involved in the youth fellowship at the church. "There are some good kids you should get to know at Christ Temple, Shane. I think it will be good for you to meet them."

I agreed to go with Uncle Erby to church the next Sunday. He went out and bought me a new suit and a white cashmere coat for the occasion. When I walked into the church, you couldn't tell me anything—I knew I was looking GOOD! In addition, I really enjoyed the service. It was so different from a Catholic mass. The people were alive and friendly; everyone, including Uncle Erby's family, was extremely nice to me.

Meanwhile, the situation with my father continued to spiral downward. His idea of good parenting was to give me a joint each morning before I left for school. In addition, the streets in his run-down neighborhood were becoming increasingly dangerous.

One day, I was standing in front of the apartment building when I saw Uncle Bucky, Uncle Erby's son, being chased down the street by several men. They pinned him against a van, took out a gun, put it to his head, and fired repeatedly, but the gun didn't go off. I ran upstairs to tell my father, but before Dad could get downstairs with his gun, the men shot Uncle Bucky and took off.

I'd heard that Uncle Bucky was on angel dust and that he was very close to losing his mind. The night before, I had seen him punch a man hard. The man fell to the pavement, hit his head, and later died. As if that were not enough trouble, the reason those men were trying to kill Uncle Bucky was that he had told a pregnant woman that he was going to cut her baby out of her body. It was the father of that baby who led the group that attacked and shot Uncle Bucky.

When my father and I got to him, Uncle Bucky was on the ground, bleeding badly from his gunshot wound. When the police and ambulance arrived, Uncle Bucky refused to go to the hospital. Afraid for Uncle Bucky's life, my father told the police about the man Uncle Bucky had assaulted the night before. Just as my father planned, Uncle Bucky was taken off the streets and into custody where he would get the medical attention he needed. Besides, with those men trying to kill him, Dad thought that Uncle Bucky would be safer in jail than on the street. My father believed he had done the right thing. Uncle Erby and Uncle Bucky did not agree.

Nothing I had ever experienced in foster care could compare to what I was now experiencing with my father. I knew that my life would go nowhere fast if I stayed with him. I was certain that before long he would have me selling drugs too. The last straw, however, was when I discovered that my father was part of a group that was stealing the identities of dead people in order to fraudulently collect their social security benefits. My father had assumed the identity of a James Patton. I can't begin to imagine the crimes he committed in Mr. Patton's name.

I was truly afraid of him now. My father had a gun, he was violent, and he wasn't even using his real name. He often threatened to hit me, but he never did, probably because of my seizures. His first wife had died of a seizure after one of their arguments, and I think he was afraid to hit me because of what had happened to her. Nevertheless, I was still afraid of him, and I began to plan my departure.

If I was going to escape without being caught, I knew I would have to outsmart one extremely nosy neighbor woman. She was always perched by her window where she could see, and ultimately report on, everything anybody did. I knew that if she saw me moving my things out, she would tell my father. To avoid suspicion, I took just a few things at a time.

That night I hailed a cab, not knowing exactly where I would go. I knew that I couldn't stay with anyone I had introduced my father to because that would make it too easy for him to find me and because I didn't want to put anyone else in danger. Once again, the Moragnes came through for me by letting me store my things at their place. When I returned to my father's apartment that evening, he didn't suspect a thing.

My plan was to escape after school the next day. The next morning, I got ready for school as usual. My father gave me the customary breakfast joint, said "See ya later, son," and out the door I went.

When the school day ended, it was time to make my getaway, but I didn't know where to go. Confused and scared, I went to Times Square to a place called Covenant House and signed myself in.

Looking at the bleak surroundings—all the mattresses on the floor and the kids sleeping on them—I decided that I just couldn't stay there. Instead, I went to the police station across the street in the Port Authority terminal and turned myself in as a runaway from foster care. I shared my story of how I had grown up in foster care and had recently run away from a group home to live with my father. I told the officer that I was now running away from my father because I wanted to go back into foster care.

I realized running away from foster care was a big mistake, and I wanted another chance. The officer pulled up their records, but I was not listed as a missing person.

"I'll be damned," I thought. The Catholic Home Bureau never even reported me missing from the foster home they had placed me in. I wondered if they even cared that I had run away.

My father was notified, and before long he and his girlfriend showed up at the police station. He told the officer that I was a pathological liar and that the whole story about being in foster care was made up. He swore to them that he had raised me and that I had a history of running away and lying. Obviously, he was very convincing because the police released me into his custody.

Driving back to Dad's place, I was terrified. He threatened me repeatedly.

"If I ever have to come to a police station again to get your ass, you won't live to regret it. Boy, I'll take you out."

At first, I just kept silent, but for some reason I made the mistake of responding to one of his threats.

"Why don't you just go ahead and do it then; just do it!"

Suddenly, he slammed on the brakes, yanked me out, and slammed me against the car. "What's wrong with you? You want me to whip your ass or something?"

He looked at me, and I just stood there paralyzed. I said not a word for fear he would smack me or do something worse. Just in time, his girlfriend Joanne jumped out of the car to intervene.

"Shane, don't say anything. Just shut up. Don't say anything."

She was able to calm my father down, and we all got back into the car without anyone getting hurt. As we continued the drive home, I became more determined than ever to get away from him.

The next morning, I rushed to school to report my situation to my counselor. At about the same time, my father finally discovered that I had moved some of my things out of his apartment. His girlfriend noticed that most of my clothes were gone, and my father saw that my typewriter was missing, too. He immediately drove to school to find me.

He entered the hallway yelling my name. I could hear him all the way down the hall in the counselor's office where I was hiding. The vice principal calmed him by threatening to call the police. After he left the building, my counselor snuck me out the back door and into a taxicab that took me to the Catholic Home Bureau. During the ride, I wondered what I could possibly say to Mr. Pointer. Surely, he wouldn't be as eager to see me again as I would be to see him. Our last meeting hadn't gone particularly well.

I tried to explain everything to Mr. Pointer and told him that I had learned my lesson. I told him that I was horribly afraid of my father. Then Mr. Pointer looked at me and asked, "What do you want us to do? We're afraid of your father too." He wanted to know why the Bureau should take me back. Why should they put their lives at risk? "Why should we do this after all you've put us through?"

I had no answer. I cried and begged them to take me back, but he was unaffected by my tears. He said he wasn't going to let me manipulate the system anymore and that they weren't going to take me back. By now, I realized I was in big trouble. I had been exposed to life with my father, and I knew it was not the life I wanted to live. I had to think of a way fast to convince the Catholic Home Bureau to take me back or else.

Finally, it dawned on me to remind Mr. Pointer that I was still a ward of the state and that he and the agency were responsible for me until I was 18 years old. "I'm not leaving until you find me a home," I declared!

6

The Storm is Over

I have been racing for years and still no
finish line. …
Every now and then, I thought I might
lose my mind.
I hollered help because I was lost.
Faith became my friend.
Then I heard a strong wind saying,
The storm is over.

—R. Kelly

The ultimatum I gave him worked out. Mr. Pointer agreed to take me back into foster care. That same day, he found a place for me in a group home in Rego Park, Queens.

Again, in search of something to ground and discipline me, I started attending Christ Temple Apostolic Church (Uncle Erby's church) every Sunday. The pastor's family would often pick me up and bring me back to the group home, because they lived in Queens too. On the way home from church one Sunday night, something happened that I can describe only as a miracle. A wintry mix of snow and sleet was falling while the pastor was driving his wife, his two daughters, and me back to Queens. As we were crossing the Queensboro Bridge, the car started sliding and spinning out of control. Because of the heavy traffic on the bridge and the severity of the spin, we were almost certain to be hit by a car or to career down a steep embankment. I just knew we were going to die.

The pastor tried desperately to get control of the car, but with no success. We were still sliding and spinning from one side of the bridge to the other when the pastor's wife said, "In the name of Jesus." The moment she spoke those words, the car came to a complete stop, facing the embankment and clear of oncoming traffic. It was nothing short of a miracle. Only God could have enabled me to survive that danger and so many other life-threatening situations. That incident went a long way toward reinforcing my faith in God.

My brush with death caused me to take a closer look at my life and to take stock of where I was and where I was going. I was sixteen years old and had only two years left as a ward of the state. Confronting the reality of my situation, I decided that it was time to get it together. I finally realized that I couldn't allow the pain and trouble I was experiencing to prevent me from achieving great things. It was time to move past the problems in my life and to focus on the opportunities that lay ahead. I needed to get myself ready for life after foster care. That meant getting serious about my education and planning a successful future.

Once I was settled into my new group home, I started taking advantage of every opportunity I was offered. Nothing was going to deter me from graduating from high school. In addition to my regular classes, I did independent study and many other things to make up the classes I had missed because I had moved around so much. I took double loads so that I could graduate on time. With every success, my self-confidence grew, but it did have a down side. Sometimes I got into fights when other residents of the group home called me church boy and punk. They thought I looked smart and my goal-oriented attitude made me different.

Because I didn't have family to visit on weekends like most of the other teens in the group home, I would sometimes spend weekends with my big brother Joe. It was always a treat when he would pick me up in his sharp, navy-blue Chrysler New Yorker and take me away from the group home for a while. Sometimes, while I was away on weekend visits or at church, the other kids would break into my room and steal things. Otherwise, my time away was enjoyable and very positive.

In spite of the conflicts while I was at Rego Park, I did manage to make some good friends who seemed to be as motivated as I was to turn their lives around. One of those friends was Kenny who, having grown up in an established white family, was sure that being in a group home with only black and Latino kids was nothing more than a bad dream. He was determined to get out of there as quickly as possible and never to look back. To make things easier on him, I agreed to become his roommate. He often referred to me as the only sane one in the group home.

In my homeroom class was a very attractive young lady named Tara. She was very slim with long, soft, bouncy hair. I was always a fool for women with pretty hair. We didn't connect right away, but that was okay because I really wanted to hook up with the most popular girl in the school, Tracy. As luck would have it, Tracy asked me out, and I jumped at the opportunity. We hit it off right away and things were going great, then suddenly Tracy became as cold as ice toward me.

When I asked her what was up, I could hardly believe her response. "I just wanted to prove to the girls that I could get you if I wanted to," she boasted. "Mission accomplished." I had no idea girls did that kind of stuff. She had no idea that she had broken my heart. I am pleased to say, however, that it was broken for only about a week—that's how long it took me to recover and start making moves toward Tara. Tara lived in a group home that was within walking distance from mine, so one day we walked home together. We liked each other from the start. We began sneaking in and out of each other's group homes just to be together, and before long she became my high school sweetheart.

While at the Rego Park group home, I was enrolled in my fifth high school, John Bowne. When the school administrators looked at my credits and absenteeism rate, they predicted that I wouldn't graduate on time. That prediction was very discouraging because I didn't want to be in the group home one day longer than I had to, and I wanted my high school diploma as soon as possible. Things started looking up, however, when I learned about Satellite Academy High, a unique school where I could complete independent study assignments that would help me make up the required credits for graduation. The school's principal assured me that I could do a lot of catching up, but he couldn't promise me that I would be able to graduate on time. I refused to be discouraged and looked forward to the challenge.

In addition to independent course work, I participated in the cooperative work-study program. This program enabled me to put money in my pocket by affording me the opportunity to work for the Federal Aviation Administration (FAA) in the Noise Abatement Office. In addition to providing spending money, that job also helped me develop a strong work ethic and gave me another opportunity to chart my own destiny. I couldn't say enough good things about Satellite Academy High. I told my roommate, Kenny, how great this school was and that I was very likely to make up my credits and graduate on time. After hearing me talk with such enthusiasm, Kenny enrolled as well.

In school, I discovered that I had the ability to lead and motivate people. I ran for president of the student government and won. Out of frustration with the quality of food and supervision at the group home, I created a newsletter called the Rego Park Post. I encouraged the other kids to submit poems or otherwise express their frustrations or observations. I typed the newsletter on my old typewriter and circulated it throughout the group home and to the foster care agency. To our amazement, the agency started listening and making the changes we wanted. We got results by channeling our energy productively! It was amazing. Maybe it was this sense of empowerment that made me look at my time with Reverend Kennedy in a different way. Although I could see the trials, I could also see his love for me, and I wrote him a letter telling him so and apologizing for all the problems I had caused him (see Appendix). He recently gave me a copy of that letter. When I read it now, I am amazed at how quickly I was maturing and at how determined I was at that time to remain in touch with my brother.

As the year progressed, it finally became clear that I would graduate on time. I was extremely relieved that I had made it in spite of everything! At the senior awards assembly, I was stunned when it was announced that I was the valedictorian of my class. Could I possibly be the smartest person in the school? *How did this happen? I wasn't as competitive about grades as the other students.* A guy who just wanted to graduate on time was graduating with honors, and I accepted the accolades with pride and dignity as Tara looked on. After attending six different high schools, three within my junior and senior years alone, I was graduating as valedictorian. The New York School of Printing, Julia Richman for the Performing Arts, St. Thomas Aquinas, Alfred E. Smith, and John Bowne were all fragments of my high school experience, but Satellite Academy was the place where I earned my diploma and the highest honor in the graduating class.

Tara and I went to the senior prom together. I wore a white tuxedo with tails. Tara was positively stunning in a lilac custom-designed satin gown and hat. We arrived in a white limousine, and when we walked in as the Prom King and Queen, everyone stopped and applauded. I felt as if I had been transformed from a frog into a prince and was living a storybook fairytale.

A whole new world was opening up for me, and the next step on my journey was college. I really needed some guidance on that subject, so I spoke with Dr. Lewis, my psychologist. Dr. Lewis suggested that I pick a small college because she thought I might find a large university overwhelming. I followed her advice, and every college I applied to accepted me. I couldn't believe so many doors were bursting wide open.

I called Mom Jenkins to give her the good news, and she could hardly believe I was graduating, let alone as valedictorian. She agreed to come to the ceremony, in part—I suspect—because she thought I was lying, and she was going to have to see it for herself.

I called my grandmother to tell her about graduation and being named valedictorian. She was extremely proud of me. I asked if she would be willing to give me a special graduation gift: the telephone number of my great-grandmother, Flossy. I knew I was asking a lot because Grandma and her mom, Flossy, did not get along at all. But it was important to me to try to have a relationship with my great-grandmother, and I wanted to invite her to my graduation. I was very grateful to Grandma for putting aside her differences long enough to give me the number. I called my great-grandmother right away, and Tara and I went to visit her.

My great-grandmother lived on the Upper West Side in Harlem. She had a beautiful apartment with imported French furniture and a player baby grand piano. "Now I know where I get my taste. It must have skipped two generations or something," I joked. We all had a good laugh. Then my great-grandmother began to talk about my mom, Sherry. Great-Grandma told me that she thought that Sherry's life would have turned out different if she had been allowed to raise Sherry. Great-Grandma had wanted very much to raise my mother, but Grandma wouldn't let her. I wondered if that was why Great-Grandma Flossy and Grandma had been estranged all these years. I wondered if things would have been different for Sherry. Would I even be here? I guess I'll never know.

Tara and I enjoyed our visit. I was very happy to have established a relationship with my great-grandmother, but there was still at least one more family rift I wanted to mend. I wanted to be reunited with my brother KB, and I asked my new social worker, Ray, to help me. Ray wasn't sure he could help me get back together with KB, but he was able to update me on what KB had been up to since I'd last seen him. I was saddened to learn that KB's adoption by Rev. Kennedy had fallen through. After that, KB went to Hillside Children's Center for a year and a half. Another couple, a Mr. and Mrs. Mills, took an interest in him and eventually adopted KB. After the adoption, Mr. and Mrs. Mills got a stern warning from Rev. Kennedy that I was a bad influence and they had better keep KB away from me.

I asked my social worker to ask the Mills if they would let me send a cassette tape that they could screen. Ray gave it a shot, and they agreed. After screening the tape, Mr. and Mrs. Mills concluded that I was anything other than a bad influence. In fact, they thought seeing me might help KB, who was acting out. They decided to send him to New York City from Rochester, New York, to attend my graduation and to give us a chance to reconnect.

Graduation day finally came, and I was reunited with KB. "It's good to see you, big brother," he said, as we embraced one another. "I'm so proud of you." It didn't matter what anyone else said or didn't say after that. As I looked out on the audience when I delivered my valedictorian's speech, I saw my grandmother, my great-grandmother, Mrs. Jenkins, and KB, and I felt as if the fibers of my life were coming back together. My grandmother started bragging about how proud she was until my great-grandmother told her, "Be quiet, the only one deserving of any credit for that boy is his mother, Mrs. Jenkins." I agreed with great-grandmother in principle, but this really was something for us all to celebrate as a family, regardless of our history and our pain. It seemed the celebration had barely started when it was time for KB to go back to Rochester. I promised to stay in touch and told him I would visit him. In fact, I decided to attend Elmira College, which was only a couple of hours away from Rochester, just to be closer to him.

Immediately after high school graduation, I worked three jobs to earn money for school. I was a file clerk at the Social Security Administration on weekdays; I served as a front desk clerk at a Best Western Hotel on weeknights, and I worked at the nightclub Justine's on weekends. Later that summer, I found out Tara was pregnant. I begged her to keep our baby, but she wouldn't. Even Tara's group home director advised her to have an abortion, and she also tried to discourage me from pursuing a romantic relationship with Tara. "You will eventually outgrow her, Shane," the director predicted. I couldn't believe that a nun was saying this and that she was encouraging Tara to have an abortion. I told Tara that I was willing to forgo Elmira College and attend Hunter

College, which was closer to her, so she, our baby, and I could be a family. I thought I had her convinced to keep the baby. But while I was working at the hotel one night, she called to inform me that she was on her way to have an abortion and that there was nothing I could do to change her mind. On that night, I vowed never to have anything to do with Tara again.

The day finally came when I left the Rego Park group home and became a freshman at Elmira College in upstate New York. I was determined to major in anything but social work, and I ultimately decided on health and human services. Maybe subconsciously I had made the decision to be a healthcare major because Ma Jenkins had gone back to school to become a registered nurse.

Things went great that first semester. New York State covered my room and board, and my tuition was covered by Pell Grants, student loans, and by a partial scholarship from Elmira. I was enjoying myself and doing well in classes. But as I was preparing to go home for the Christmas break, I realized something: I had no home to go back to. All my college friends were making plans to go home to spend time with their families. Meanwhile, the group home had given away my room to a new resident. The staff did, however, offer me the option of sleeping on their couch. The situation was a painful reminder that abused and neglected children who overcome tremendous challenges and manage, against all odds, to survive the foster care system, end up without a home. It didn't seem right for them, and it certainly didn't feel right for me. There was, I concluded, something very wrong with the system.

It was a great comfort when Mr. and Mrs. Mills, who had adopted my brother KB, invited me to be a part of their family. After I had explained how disheartening it was not to receive mail at school, Ma Mills had started sending me care packages, and I stayed with the Mills family during holidays. It was a relief to have a place to call home again, and gradually the sick feeling that I got every semester break when friends would start talking about their families began subsiding.

I didn't bother to explain to my classmates that I had been a foster child; I just claimed Mom and Dad Mills as my parents too. It felt good to say that my dad was an associate professor at SUNY Brockport and that my mom was the Minority Business Enterprise Officer for the city of Rochester. When I needed to learn to drive, Dad Mills taught me in his Chevy Malibu, and that felt great!

But calling someone Mom and Dad and being able to count on them when trouble comes are two different things. One night I was returning from a trip to New York City when my car broke down in the mountains of upstate New York. It was so late, and I was still so far from Rochester that I didn't feel I could call the Mills family. There was no one else to contact, but I was fortunate enough to get help from a stranger who put me up for the night, paid for my ruined tire, and sent me on my way the next morning. I shudder to think what might have happened if I hadn't been so lucky.

College life continued to go well. I stayed at Elmira College for the first two years, then applied to Morehouse College and was accepted. However, some unexpected news threatened to derail my train. Tara and I had tried unsuccessfully to get back together, but her visit to Elmira a few months earlier had resulted in another pregnancy. She was three months along, and this time I was determined that she wasn't going to have an abortion. The situation was further complicated by the fact that, since things were supposedly over between Tara and me, I had fallen madly in love with Janice, a fellow Elmira student. Janice was not only one of the prettiest young ladies on campus, but she was also one of the smartest. Janice's first reaction to the pregnancy news was that we would survive it. She understood my foster care history and knew how much I'd want to be there for my kid. But being a dad from a distance was not acceptable to me. I told Janice that we had to end our relationship so that Tara and I could have a chance for the baby's sake. Janice said she understood, and we said our good-byes. If getting pregnant was Tara's way of getting us back together, it worked. Because of her and the baby, I decided not to go to Morehouse.

My big brother Joe was outraged. He told me that I'd be throwing my life away if I didn't insist that Tara abort the baby. I didn't agree. I could not sanction aborting my child, because every time I looked in the mirror I was reminded of how close my mother came to aborting me. I also remembered God's intervention on my behalf. Instead, I enlisted in the Navy's BOOST program, which would eventually make me a commissioned officer. This enlistment was my way of ensuring that our baby would not have to go through the things I went through. Joining the service allowed me to provide for my wife and child and to finish my education at the same time.

I was scheduled to leave for the Navy's BOOST program on June 28, but the baby was due between June 28 and July 5. Although I wanted to be present for the delivery, securing my family's future seemed more important. Tara didn't agree. She wanted me there when she gave birth, so I met with my recruiter and forfeited my slot in BOOST and my opportunity to obtain a commission. After I received my associate's degree on June 5 from Elmira College, Tara and I left for New York City.

My old Volkswagen had worn-out shock absorbers, and the bumpy ride back to New York might have caused Tara to go into labor. In any case, on June 8, three to four weeks before she was due, Tiffany Monique Salter was born at about 12:30 a.m. Tara and I were both 19. Tiffany was born crying and shivering, but when the nurse placed her in my arms, the shivering and crying stopped. As a tear fell from my eye, I looked into hers and promised her that she would never know the pain I had known. Everything I did from that day forward was for my precious baby girl.

After Tiffany was born, Tara went to live in a teen mom and baby program. Before I left for the Navy, we were secretly married. I wanted to be sure that Tiffany never felt illegitimate if I lost my life in combat.

My departure date for the Navy was now September 23. Meanwhile, I quickly took the best-paying job I could find in New York City, which was in the housekeeping department of a Jewish nursing home. As a union member, I was actually making more money mopping, waxing, and buffing floors than many of the administrative assistants earned. I wore a gray housekeeping uniform, which I found humbling because I had just graduated from college. People in the building usually didn't speak to me when I wore that uniform. When they turned up their noses, I would mumble under my breath, "I probably make more money than you anyway." Because of the terrible way I was treated, I made a promise that I would never look down on anyone because of that person's job. I worked as many hours as they would give me, just to be sure that Tiffany and Tara were well taken care of.

When September 23 came, I left for boot camp in San Diego, California, as planned. Just a few weeks into boot camp, Tara wrote me saying, "I'm tired of you being away. If this is the way our life is going to be, then I want a divorce." What was I to do? I didn't want to be in boot camp getting my butt whipped in the blazing heat. I was there only because I had a family that needed instant income security. It was our ticket out of the foster care system for certain. How could she send me that kind of letter? *Damn, how dare she? Here I go again*, I thought. *Not in my adult life, too! Right out the gate, I'm trying to create my own family, and she's ready to walk out on me just like everyone else.* I wanted to throw in the towel right there and say, "Forget it." I asked myself what this fight was really for and how much more I would have to put up with. I wondered if anyone ever hung in with you for the long haul, and I almost started feeling sorry for myself. Then I looked at a picture of Tiffany, and suddenly everything was all right. The struggle was for Tiffany, my baby girl, so she would not have to pay for the sins of her parents the rest of her life.

I wrote back to Tara and told her never to send me a letter like that again. I reminded her that I was getting my ass kicked in boot camp for her and Tiffany, and I didn't need that kind of distraction. Later, I learned that the letter was Tara's way of letting me know she was having an affair. I believe her affair resulted in her third pregnancy, even though she claimed I was the father. Apparently Tara found out she was pregnant again a few weeks after I left for boot camp, and for the second time she had an abortion.

I was determined to complete boot camp and become a hospital corpsman. That experience would enable me to provide for my family and ultimately to become a hospital administrator. To reach my goal, I had to re-enroll in college immediately after boot camp. I could see myself running a clinic, overseeing a department within a medical facility, or maybe even serving as the CEO of a hospital somewhere. I had big dreams, and I had a plan. But my plan was seriously threatened when I couldn't pass my swim test. After failing for the fourth time, I wrote Tara and said, "I may not make it. They are threatening to kick me out if I don't pass the next time. If they do, I guess I'll try the Air Force." Thank God, I passed the next time, and my Navy career was back on track.

I had been proud when I graduated from high school as valedictorian, but that was nothing compared to the pride I felt when I graduated from boot camp. As we marched and the band played the National Anthem, I got chills up my spine. I had officially become one of America's own. I finally belonged somewhere. I had an identity as a sailor in the United States Navy. After graduating, I remained in San Diego for the rest of the year, where I completed requirements to become a hospital corpsman. I was asked to list the top three places I wanted to be stationed. My first choice was Charleston, South Carolina, because I heard it was a big Navy town, which would be a lot of fun. It also wasn't too far from Tara's mother in Hilton Head. My second choice was the National Naval Medical Center in Bethesda, Maryland, because I was told was where the big brass was and that if I were noticed there, it could really propel my career. I ended up in Bethesda. While stationed there, I completed my rotation on the in-patient wards, working deadly rotating shifts.

I did so well that, in record time, I petitioned to be assigned to a clinic so I could go back to school. My petition was honored, and I was assigned for the next few years to the Pediatric Acute Care Clinic. I enrolled in the base's external degree program through Southern Illinois University at Carbondale, majoring in healthcare management. Eventually, I became the senior corpsman in the clinic, and my superiors strongly encouraged me to enroll in the Armed Forces Medical School to become a physician. My commander, who was impressed with my ambition and clinical skills, said that if I wanted it, he would make it happen.

Well, I knew I did not want to be a physician bad enough to endure all that I would have to endure to get there. Second, I knew that Tara's support was weak, at best. Tara resented the amount of time I spent on my studies. We were about twenty years old, and

Tara felt we should be clubbing more and having an active social life. I promised her that socializing would come in time, and I tried to convince her that my education was an investment in our future. She obviously was not very committed to our marriage. Shortly after being assigned to the pediatric clinic and relocating Tara and Tiffany from New York, I found an unmailed love letter she had written to another man. As much as I wanted to create my own family, my ego could not handle the affair, and I asked for a divorce. It was ugly. We fought and fought a long time before agreeing to go our separate ways.

Initially, we agreed that I would have custody of Tiffany. Then Tara suddenly changed her mind, and I was devastated. She figured she could get money from me if she took Tiffany with her. To further complicate our impending separation, Tara was pregnant again. Despite my objections, Tara decided to have another abortion. "I'll have a better chance of finding someone with one child than with two," she said. At that point, for the first time, I actually wanted her to have an abortion. I even gave her the money for it. I was, however, quite devastated to learn later that we had aborted twins.

The day Tara left with my baby girl, my world shattered. I refused to fight for custody because I didn't want to establish a precedent for her to use Tiffany as a way to get at me. To add salt to the wound, Tara decided that they would move to Hilton Head, South Carolina, to live with Tara's mother. She knew how much I loved Tiffany. Why would she move so far away? Why wouldn't she just go back to New York, which I could get to in four hours?

Shortly after Tara left, I moved into a townhouse with two roommates. One weekend, I planned a drive to New York to visit Joe and to show him my new car. I called a couple of nights before, to confirm that I was coming but got no answer. I found that odd because, as a senior employee at Western Electric, he had instant access to the latest technological equipment. Surely he, at least, had an answering machine. After not being able to get in touch with him, I decided to postpone the trip until I could be sure Joe was in town.

The next Tuesday, the Red Cross summoned me. When I arrived at the Red Cross offices, they told me that Joe had been robbed and killed in New York. Now I had another reason to hate New York. My head was still spinning as I learned that Joe was going to be buried the next day. I booked the first flight available, but it was delayed and I missed the funeral. A friend picked me up at the airport and rushed me to the cemetery. Joe's casket had already been laid in the ground. I never had the chance to see him again or to say good bye to him.

The pain was even deeper than when I learned of my mother's death. I was devastated. My big brother—mentor, friend, and confidante—was gone. I made my way to where the family had gathered after Joe's funeral and spoke with a friend of Joe's, who told me that I should never try to find a replacement for Joe in my life because there never would be one. That was the best advice he could have given me. No one understood me like Joe, no one motivated me like Joe, and no one loved me like Joe. Every day of my life, I still miss him. He was my hero. I wish he could see the man I've become. He'd be pleased to know I hung in there in spite of it all.

A year later, my ex-wife called and said that she could no longer provide for Tiffany and asked me to take permanent custody. What was I supposed to do? I was living with two other guys in a three-bedroom town house in Silver Spring, Maryland, but I couldn't let that stand in the way. Somehow, I worked it out with Zarick and Jesse to have Tiffany come live with us for a while. Tiffany and I would share the same room at first, but shortly after she arrived, Zarick moved out and Tiffany got her own room.

Tiffany was two years old when I got custody of her. Even as a single parent, I was determined that she would have the life of a princess. She went with me everywhere. Eventually, Tiffany and I were able to get our own place in Rockville, Maryland. To finish my degree and earn additional income, I had girlfriends watching Tiffany in shifts. I was enrolled in school full-time, was working part-time, and was fulfilling my last year in the Navy.

After I completed my four years in the Navy, I didn't reenlist. On the day of my discharge, I stood in front of the National Naval

Medical Center with Tiffany beside me. "Here in Maryland is where we will plant our roots," I vowed. "We will redefine what it means to be a Salter."

I decided that I would transition from Navy active duty to Air Force Reserve. Now to many people that didn't make much sense because the Navy and the Air Force are not at all similar, but that difference made it more exciting for me. I was always intrigued by the Air Force. I was offered a position as an entry-level supervisor at Children's Hospital in Washington, D.C., and I joined the Air Force Reserve.

My Air Force experience only confirmed how much more I liked the Navy, and I privately questioned the logic of my decision to join the Air Force until I met a sweet, unassuming young lady. She had a radiant smile and never was a strand of hair out of place. As far as substance goes, she was the most solid woman I'd ever met. At first, I wasn't interested in her romantically—I didn't think she was my type—but I certainly wanted her to be my friend.

After promising month after month to call her, I ran into her and struck up a conversation about a challenge I was facing. Tiffany was about to be christened. The sleeves on her beautiful white christening dress were too long, and I did not know how to sew. Gloria agreed to take the dress home and alter it for me. After the christening, I invited her over for dinner with Tiffany and me as a gesture of gratitude. That was the night I discovered that Gloria was adopted. Even though her adoption experience was considerably different from mine, I felt she identified with me on some level.

7

Love, Daddy

My children, I wish these things for you...
a family that has a special place for each
one's gentle little face.
Parents who lift your self-esteem, while
nurturing the potential of your dreams.
Love that comes from me to you,
these things I wish your whole life
through.
You see, my children, when I was small
I didn't feel much love at all.
I grew up in so much pain while other
children scorned my name
and all the adults that were supposed to
protect me, never stayed, never kept me.
So here's my chance to give to you
those precious things I wanted too.
They are the things I hold so dear,
a family built with love that is sincere.
One day you will understand my pain,
but more important the love I gave.
 I know you'll love your children too—
the way your daddy always loved you.
Remember, some things I never knew,
until the day God gave me you.

—Love, Daddy
S. Salter

Gloria and I became good friends at first, and then one day I realized that I was romantically attracted to her. I realized something had changed for me when she tried to hook me up with a friend of hers who was not even in her league. Right after that setup, I expressed my interest in Gloria, and we started dating. I was having a real hard time getting up the nerve for that first kiss. Then my friend Harold told me, you had better kiss that woman before she thinks something is wrong with you. Well, the pressure was on. We were standing by the car saying good bye after a date one night, while Tiffany waited in the back seat, when I finally kissed Gloria. Tiffany was so excited that she called her "Mommy." That's when Gloria did something that truly impressed me. She said to Tiffany, "I'm not your mother, sweetie," and gave her a hug. She took an awkward situation and handled it directly, yet with great sensitivity.

After that first kiss, I knew I wanted to marry Gloria, but I hadn't filed for divorce from Tara. I had told Tara that if she wanted a divorce, she was going to pay for it. I didn't have much money, and what I did have was for Tiffany. I had told Tara to just file, and I wouldn't contest it. After taking such a stance, I knew if I sent her divorce papers, she would know something was up and become obstructive just for the hell of it. Gloria made it clear to me that I shouldn't even think about proposing to her until my divorce was final. Well, under the circumstances, I thought I might have to wait for years. Then a few weeks later, a miracle happened. Unsolicited, divorce papers arrived from an attorney in South Carolina who was representing Tara. I took the arrival of those papers as a sign. Gloria was the woman for me, and she was the stepmother Tiffany deserved.

Right away, I started preparing to purchase a ring, and again Gloria dropped a gentle hint. "If you need help paying for it, let me know," she said. I interpreted that as code for "Don't bring me a diamond chip, nothing less than half a karat will do."

I couldn't stop laughing, but I also got the message. I found a great ring, I proposed, and Gloria accepted.

Meanwhile, my little brother KB had been living with me for almost a year. KB said his plan was to go into the service, but I don't think those were ever his true intentions. I leveraged my reputation and relationships to get him a job at Children's Hospital, only to see him terminated within the first month. Fortunately, not many people knew he was my brother, and the embarrassment was minimal.

KB took every opportunity to remind me of the pain he endured after I left him behind in Rochester. "Enough already," I remember saying. "How many times are we going to talk about this?" I tried repeatedly to explain that I made the best decision I could under the circumstances. "For crying out loud, I was fifteen," I shouted! This underlying issue remains unresolved for him to this day. Every other conversation between the two of us circles back to when I left him behind at age twelve in Rochester.

Once, the tension between us escalated to a fistfight in my apartment. A few inches taller than me, he thought he could whip me, but I was determined to show him otherwise. Given our history, our relationship should have never deteriorated to a physical confrontation. Our rage was intense, and I was afraid that future fights might lead to the death of one of us. Because witnessing such violent encounters could be detrimental to five-year-old Tiffany, I asked KB to leave.

KB moved to Washington, D.C., angry with me and very uncertain about where he belonged. He resolved to survive by any means necessary. I would hear from him from time to time, but our relationship had become increasingly strained. It was challenging, but we never lost sight of the fact that we were brothers and loved each other very much. Therefore, when KB called in need of a place to stay, I offered my apartment. It was getting close to my wedding day, so Tiffany and I were spending most of our time at Gloria's anyway. I gave KB my apartment, fully furnished, with the understanding that he would pay the utilities. KB was elated, and I was glad that I could do something to help him, but it turned out to be a big mistake. I went by the apartment one day to pack some of my things and was shocked to find it filthy. The electricity hadn't been paid, the lights had been turned off, and the refrigerator was completely defrosted. As if that were not enough, I walked into Tiffany's room to find her ceramic piggy bank shattered into a million pieces and all of the money we had been saving since her birth was gone. At that moment, my heart was shattered into a million pieces too. He couldn't have hurt me more if he had tried.

I couldn't find KB for weeks, but he resurfaced just before the wedding. Originally, he was supposed to be a groomsman, but I did not want to rely on him for a role that wasn't easily replaceable, so I asked him to perform the less demanding task of escorting distinguished guests down the aisle. He was supportive and agreed. Meanwhile, Gloria and I had already started house shopping. We found a beautiful home in Fort Washington, Maryland, on almost two acres of land, and we were able to move in a few months before the wedding.

The day arrived for me to marry the woman who had become my best friend. Ebenezer A.M.E. Church in Fort Washington, Maryland, was beautifully decorated for the occasion. KB escorted Gloria's adoptive mother down the aisle. Despite several knee surgeries and having to use a walker, she was determined to make that walk. Representing me were three sets of parents: Mom and Dad Mills, Mom and Dad Moragne, and Mom Jenkins. Pop Jenkins was not able to make it, but Robbie Jenkins was there. I was so glad to see my foster brother! My grandmother was there too, beaming with pride along with my mother's baby brother, Uncle Pierre. My mom's sister, Jewel, who was now the latest family casualty of drug addiction, used the occasion to create a scene. She demanded a rose and insisted on someone escorting her down the aisle like an official member of the bridal party. I'm sure the entire church could hear her yelling in the vestibule, "I am his dead mother's sister and I should be given her props." Jewel refused to be quiet until one of the hostesses took the rose off her garment and pinned it on Jewel's dress. Then KB escorted her down the aisle.

With all the drama behind us, I was finally—after so many years—going to have the family I had always dreamed of. Attired in his Air Force dress blues, Technical Sergeant Douglas Bell almost stole the show as he rolled out the red carpet in cadence. The sight of my sister, Shanique, who was a junior bridesmaid, and Tiffany, who was the flower girl, brought tears to my eyes. Those initial tears were just the beginning of my emotions, however, because when Gloria walked in, no one came close to her radiance. For the first time, nothing about my past mattered because our future was so bright. I was on my way to building the family for Tiffany and me that had existed, until then, only in my dreams.

A year later, our first child together, Brittney Nicole, was born. Gloria and I learned in advance that we were having a girl, and while I tried not to let it show, this time I had really hoped for a boy. After sixteen hours of labor, the baby's heart rate was dropping, and the doctor decided to perform an emergency caesarean section. When Brittney emerged, she was blue and not breathing. At that moment, I thought I was being punished for wanting a boy instead of just being thankful for a healthy baby. In that minute, I prayed to God to save our baby and spare my wife. "She doesn't deserve this. Please save our baby," I pleaded. Within minutes, Brittney was breathing.

After our second daughter, Courtney Shanade, was born a few years later, we realized that if we were going to have sons, they would have to be adopted.

Our first son, Rico Giovanni, came to us at the age of six. Rico was biracial—too dark for white families, and was considered undesirable by most black families. The combination of his race and his age classified him as hard to place. However, he was anything but undesirable to Gloria and me. We couldn't wait to see him.

Our first meeting was so exciting, and I couldn't get over the fact that he looked so much like me. The agency told me that, although he had been diagnosed with separation anxiety as a preschooler, he had responded well to treatment and was a well-adjusted kid. He was wearing checkered pants and a striped shirt with a coat full of dirt and grease. We wondered what kind of foster home sends a child to meet prospective parents dressed like that. Perhaps one with a strategic agenda. If the child looks pathetic, the prospective parents might feel overwhelmed with sympathy and move quickly to get him out of there. Gloria and I instantly decided that he would join our family.

During his first pre-placement weekend visit with us, Rico's responses to questions seemed programmed. For example, if I asked him why he was doing something he shouldn't have been doing, his response was "because I'm bad." It became clear that these obviously programmed responses were meaningless to him. I also noticed that he sometimes struggled to understand questions. I wondered if he was hard of hearing.

Gloria and I met with Rico's teachers, hoping they could shed some light on his behavior. The teacher we spoke to showed us Rico's consistent A and B coursework. She knew him well and was certain that all he needed was to be adopted. "Please give him a home. He is so sweet; he just needs a good home," she said.

My heart ached for him, just as my heart ached when I was in Rico's shoes as a little boy hoping that someone would give me a home. They brought him into the classroom that day dressed in purple corduroy pants that seemed to be about two sizes too small. All I could think about was getting him some new clothes and trashing those tight purple pants. He must have been humiliated dressed like that. Later that day, we met his foster parents, who reminded me of the Balfours. Just like the Balfours, Rico's foster mother did not intend to adopt him, but they had adopted a little girl that came into their home after Rico. The original plan to reunite Rico with his birth father didn't work out, and this event had cleared the way for us to become his family.

Rico made it clear that he didn't like his name and wanted to be named after me. I couldn't have been prouder, and I could certainly understand why he associated belonging and security with his name. However, I told him that one of the few things he had received from his birth mother was his name and that I thought he should keep part of it. Therefore, he became Shane Lenard Rico Salter Jr. and I added Rico to my name to become Shane Lenard Rico Salter Sr.

Shortly after he came to us, I noticed he was having difficulties in school. At first, I figured the problems had arisen because he was still adjusting to life with us. However, when things didn't seem to get any better, I made an appointment with the Department of Psychiatry and Speech Pathology at Children's Hospital where I worked as hospital administrator. The psychologist gave us several diagnoses, but his major problem was receptive language disorder, which is similar to dyslexia. Gloria and I addressed his needs through special education services and in-home therapy. The following year, Shane Rico's adoption became final.

Shane Rico had always had trouble controlling his anger. From the start, we went to great lengths to reassure him that we were his family and that we were never going to give up on him no matter how many problems he had. The more we reassured him that he was loved and this home was it, the easier it was for him to let go of the hurt and anger that had built up over the years. Thanks to Shane Rico, we had too many busted walls and windows to count over the years. I found it interesting that Shane Rico would do most of his damage when I wasn't in the house. Tiffany would always say, "Dad, he acts very different when you're not home."

I rather naively tried to write it off as normal behavior. I believed that he behaved differently around me and always wanted to be with me because he felt that I was the only one who understood him. I'd been in his shoes before, and I did everything I could to let him know I accepted him unconditionally. He had also never had a man in his life. I think that having lived in a foster home with sisters and a foster mom who didn't adopt him after six years, he was guarded against gestures of love and commitment from women, and he never deeply bonded with his new mom and sisters, although he enjoyed them.

He was such a likable kid. There was no reason for him not to fit in, but he didn't. He was too focused, serious, and intense. I began to notice Shane Rico didn't enjoy the things other children his age enjoyed. He didn't like to play with groups of other children (he couldn't handle the give-and-take), but he liked being with one friend at a time and had his own set of pleasures. On one occasion, as we were crossing a bridge in the car, he jumped with excitement at the beauty and magnitude of the open body of water. He just took it all in and enjoyed the moment.

I identified with him. As a child, the nuns in Catholic School always punished me for my difficulties with social behavior, and I remember how great it felt just sitting with Dad Jenkins watching

"60 Minutes" instead of trying to play with other kids and toys. I was always a loner: intense, serious, and living life with purpose. Unlike Shane Rico, I was able to develop a superficial extraverted personality to survive, but it had nothing to do with whom I really am.

Shane Rico and I looked forward to our special moments while we were driving. He would ask me questions about everything, and we'd sing our favorite song _"All by myself ... don't want to be ... all by myself any more ..."_ We would sing that song on the way to the store, on the way to school, and even when we went fishing. We always sang. He would crack up watching me acting out some of the lyrics to other songs every now and then. Each time I'd say, "Hold on, that's my favorite song." One day, Shane Rico "busted" me and said, "Dad, they're all your favorite songs." I guess he was right. I love music and so does he.

Shane Rico had been in foster care since the age of one-year. His father was an alcoholic, and his mother suffered from schizophrenia. We were told that he was predisposed, but we didn't know that sons of schizophrenic mothers were at higher risk than daughters. Truthfully, I don't think it would have made a difference to our decision. We thought it was possible, not probable, and we never watched for it or thought about it again. He was a challenging child from the beginning, but he was my first son, so I thought he was different from the girls because he had more testosterone.

Unfortunately, the holes in our walls were getting larger with each new outburst, and I started to realize that Shane Rico was having more than just a little trouble handling his anger. His tantrums grew more frequent, and he started getting angry for no reason (for example, if somebody just looked at him wrong). The other children in the family started warning me, saying, "You should see the way he looks at Mom sometimes when you're gone; he looks at her like he's gonna snap when she tells him to do something."

I thought back to my anger and rage when I was a kid but couldn't identify with this. His behavior seemed extreme at times—especially the day when he was confronted about something he did and reacted by flying off to his room and putting his fist through the window. He was ten years old at the time, but I almost kicked his you know what. "Have you lost your mind?" I asked him.

Shortly afterwards, we had to hospitalize him for depression. He was flat, didn't want to play, and didn't respond to anything. My concern grew deeper when one night Gloria did a bed check, and he wasn't there. She searched the house and finally found him playing with candles. He had put all of our lives in jeopardy. Desperate times call for desperate measures. We looked at each other and declared we needed help. We called a meeting at school and got him a new Individualized Educational Plan (IEP), which called for intensive psychological support services in the classroom and a smaller class size. Through Prince George's County, we received in-home counseling as well, but not much progress was made.

Shane Rico was twelve when our second son, David, arrived. We thought that having a brother—one who was also adopted—would take the pressure off him, but instead his outbursts seemed to escalate.

I had received a call from a friend who worked at the local child and family services agency, telling me the agency had a kid who would be perfect for our family. The child had been featured on a local television newscast, and my friend sent me a copy of the videotape. As soon as Gloria and I saw it, we fell in love with 14-year-old David.

Grandma was visiting at the time so I asked her what she thought. She said, "If I could raise six, you can raise five." Probably not the best response to listen to, I thought.

I asked Tiffany about her feelings and she responded just as a teenage girl would, "He's cute. I'll be very popular at school."

For me, the most moving part of the tape was David's response when the reporter asked why, at fourteen, David still wanted to be adopted. "When I'm thirty years old, I'm going to want a place to bring my children back to," David said.

I was thirty at the time, and I had no place to bring my children back to. I felt an instant connection to him. The rest of the family saw the tape, we talked it over, and everybody agreed that David should become a part of our family. It was a unanimous decision. We didn't tell any of our friends or extended family right away because we thought they would try to discourage us from adopting a black teenage boy, especially with three girls at home. Born David Lewis, our son became David Lenard Aytch Salter, and Gloria and I were thrilled that we were able to give a home to another child branded "hard to place."

When my father-in-law found out about our plans, he said, "What the hell are you trying to do to my daughter? Don't you all have enough kids?" I told him that he was selling himself short if he believed he had raised a child who wasn't an independent thinker. In fact, it was the gift of adoption he had given her that compelled her to give that gift to others. He never uttered a word on the subject again.

Months later, Grandma agreed to come down from New York to watch the children so Gloria and I could take a trip together. The two of us hadn't had a break together in years. Finding someone to watch the kids for any length of time, since neither one of us has an extended family, was next to impossible. It's one reason we wanted a big family. We hoped our children would support each other when they became adults. Thank God for Grandma. She seemed to always be there when we needed her. No excuses—just there. If Gloria was in the hospital for minor surgery, Grandma was there to nurse her back to health. If Gloria was out of town on business, Grandma would come down to give me a hand because she knew I was hopeless without my wife.

As young as Grandma claimed to be, her true age was beginning to show. I was reluctant even to ask her to watch the children, but we really needed this respite. Off we went to Texas—a business trip for Gloria with me along for company. We weren't gone more than 24 hours when the telephone rang. It was Grandma calling from our house to inform us that there was a big problem. In the background, I could hear glass smashing onto the floor and objects crashing against the wall. Shane Rico was out of control. I instructed her to have David contain him and call the police. Never could I have imagined that I would call the police on my own child, but it was necessary to protect him and everyone else in the house.

When the police arrived, I told them over the phone that, because my wife and I were away, my son needed to be removed from the house. The police officer said they would take him to the Juvenile Detention Center. Then, at my request, they put my son on the phone. He was sobbing uncontrollably. With as reassuring a tone as I could muster, I told him we would straighten everything out when I got home but for now, because he could not keep himself safe, he had to go with the policeman. Like a wounded lamb, he said okay. The next morning, I was on a plane headed home. David did all he could to clean up the evidence of Shane Rico's rage, but there was no hiding it. Everything had changed, and our family would never be the same.

Our medical insurance would not cover the long-term residential treatment that Shane Rico needed. After moving from Prince George's County, Maryland, where services were abundant but the schools were second best, to Chantilly, Virginia, in Fairfax County, where the schools were good but services were nonexistent, we were told by a social worker that Shane Rico would get the comprehensive help he needed only if he was charged and convicted of assaulting his siblings. Then the county would be obligated to help us by using the Family Resource Assistance Team. When I arrived at the courthouse, the detective assured me that having him adjudicated would enable him to receive comprehensive psychiatric services. *What's that about? Let's lock him up to make him eligible for treatment? What's the real motivation here?* I should have been much more suspicious when the court social worker asked me, "Why would you want to keep a kid like this anyway?"

"Why?" I responded, "Because he's my kid!"

When I read Shane Rico's record, the social worker had written in the notes that I hadn't resolved my foster care issues. She didn't expect me to read that, I'm sure. Unfortunately, I saw it after I agreed to let them charge my son as a criminal. To see him hauled away in handcuffs was heartbreaking for both his mother and me.

As a parent, I was ashamed, was remorseful, and felt that I had failed him.

What was even worse, none of the services promised were ever delivered. After attending meeting after meeting, opening ourselves up to inquiry after inquiry as if Shane Rico were the only child we had at home and adhering to the requirements of the county, attending meetings and hearings, our son received not one county service. In fact, the County demanded that the District of Columbia pay for his care under the adoption subsidy agreement (which the city initially refused to honor) and threatened to remand Shane Rico to foster care and to come after us for his board if D.C. did not come through. The latter option would have bankrupted us and put the rest of the children at risk.

This could not be happening, I thought. I went to District of Columbia Child and Family Services, which was under receivership at the time, and threatened to call a press conference unless they followed through with the services promised. The staff reexamined their obligation under the subsidy agreement and decided that it was in all of our best interests for them to honor it. The agency has since had a leadership change and is now being administered by a very capable and energetic visionary.

We ultimately found Kids Peace for Children in Crisis in Allentown, Pennsylvania. We visited and decided that the atmosphere and treatment program would help Shane Rico, so we transferred him there. It was hard making six-hour round trips between Virginia and Pennsylvania every other weekend, but we refused to miss any scheduled visits. After several years, we found a treatment facility much closer to home.

I wanted a sign from Shane Rico that he wanted to come back home, but he barely progressed through the different levels of his treatment program. Finally, I asked myself if we had let this situation go on too long and if he was now more comfortable in an institution than with us. Even though he repeatedly declared that he looked forward to coming home someday, as soon as he had progressed far enough to earn home privileges, he would have a setback. It looked like self-sabotage to me. No matter what, we were determined to remain his parents and to continue visiting him indefinitely if that's what it took. Fortunately, now that he was closer, we could see him every Sunday, and sometimes during the week. It was not unusual for Gloria to drop by for lunch when her schedule permitted.

Over time, we noticed significant improvement in his behavior. I'm sure the increased visits had plenty to do with that. He started earning passes for home visits but, unbelievably, his probation officer would not authorize him to leave the facility. I hit the roof. "That's where I draw the line," I remember saying. I informed the hospital that I was no longer authorizing the probation officer to review any information in my son's medical record if that review was going to be used for punitive reasons that were a direct contradiction to his therapeutic needs. Well, that was the beginning of the next world war. I had no idea what I was in for. The probation officer subpoenaed me into court along with the CEO of the hospital. Cash-strapped from other associated expenses, I entered the courtroom with only faith as my legal counsel.

The county attorney represented Shane Rico. I thought it was amusing that my son had an attorney, but I was there protecting his interests without one. The probation officer pleaded his case to the judge regarding the importance of access to his medical records, and I responded with our view of the situation.

The judge began lecturing me from the bench, saying that probation was the only way that a sixteen-year-old child was going to comply with treatment.

After initially being polite and not getting my point across, I thought I had nothing to lose. I interrupted the judge and said, "Your Honor, you are obviously not hearing me."

There was dead silence in the courtroom. Even I thought to myself, "*Oh*"... but I got the courage to continue and said, "That's what he has parents for." I then reminded the judge that we had brought this matter before the court, and that the only reason we had done so was to try to get him the care he needed. "Well, your Honor," I went on to say, "he hasn't received any of the care they promised, and I'm asking you, in light of those facts, to close this case."

It was obvious that the judge was caught off guard. "You mean the incident happened in your home?"

"Yes, Your Honor," I replied.

"You brought the matter before the court?"

"Yes, Your Honor."

With gavel in hand, he uttered, "Case dismissed!"

A loud outburst from Gloria was heard, and she started to cry. The CEO of the hospital was crying as well. They kept saying I was awesome. I felt like some kind of hero for a minute, but I knew who the real hero was. It was someone much bigger than me. This was a miracle. I could not even remember what I said, or where the words came from. I was happy that a wrong was made right, and all of those county workers were finally out of our lives. We could now focus exclusively on our son's healing.

I was downright angry for many days. At first, I asked God, "Why me? Why—after all that I have already been through in my own childhood—would You have me endure this with an adopted son?" I asked God how He could expect me to continue to motivate people to adopt when we had had such a traumatic experience.

After years of agony and pain, the answer came. There was purpose in my pain. It was very easy, given all that I had experienced as a child in foster care, to ask people to adopt or give a child what I had never had and always wanted. But having lived through an adoption experience that included love, disappointment, heartache, and triumph, I could now go out and say, "When it's at its worst, don't you dare give up! You may get tired, you might burn out and have to take a break, but don't you dare give up! You may have to parent some of our special-needs adopted children unconventionally, just as you would a special-needs birth child that can't be cared for at home, but don't ever stop being a parent!" That was the powerful lesson my experience with Shane Rico Jr. taught me.

Shane Rico is now an adult, working with computers, living in New York, and doing unbelievably well. It meant the world to him to know that, although he wasn't able to live at home, he mattered to someone. He knew he had a family who cared enough to come visit him consistently, to advocate for him vigorously, and to love him unconditionally. Every child deserves at least that much. Considering everything he's had to overcome to get where he is, I am so proud of Shane Rico. So many people his age have had so much more and have thrown it away. Shane Rico is using everything he has and is making the most of it.

In the middle of Shane Rico's drama, my brother KB came to stay with us in exchange for helping around the house and watching the children. It turned out to be not quite that simple. I received a call alerting me that my other brother, my father's son David, had been arrested in New York. This incident was of particular concern to me because, two years before, I had driven up for David's junior high school graduation when he was fourteen. During that time, I had tried everything to convince his grandmother to let him move in with me. I was deeply troubled by the crowd he was associating with and by his defeatist attitude. This concern was heightened when someone asked him after graduation where his father was. I quietly watched as David responded, "He's dead."

I asked him why he said that, and he replied, "You could come all the way from Maryland, Shane, but our so-called father couldn't come from Harlem up to the Bronx for my graduation." Dad's absence hurt David deeply. Each promise our father made and didn't keep had taken a toll. David was becoming increasingly sad, hopeless, and filled with rage. His capacity to dream of life beyond the projects of Mott Haven was diminished by the countless number of hardened friends he associated with. I told his grandmother, Ms. Jones, that it was time for him to be around a consistent positive male role model, but she refused to let him live with me. She needed him to help with his two other sisters and his cousin, who were also being raised in her two-bedroom apartment. David was now sixteen and had already been arrested. He was almost certainly on his way to Rikers Island.

We were at a crossroads. David was no longer listening to his grandmother. He was coming and going as he pleased, and now he was facing jail time. I went to New York to speak to the judge on his behalf. I promised the court that New York would never have a problem with David again if the judge would allow me the chance to intervene. I asked him to release David into my custody and to let him move with me to Maryland. The judge said yes, and finally David's grandmother agreed to let him live with my family.

Soon after David's arrival, Gloria and I learned that he drank very heavily almost every day. Such behavior was, of course, unacceptable. We enrolled him in a G.E.D. program. We also monitored his every movement, which prompted him to call his grandmother and tell her that he thought I hated him. However, unlike my brother KB, David responded to my attempts to get him on track. We agreed that he would not work because we wanted his focus to be on getting his diploma. That agreement made him miserable, but it paid off. David passed his G.E.D on his first attempt.

After he got his G.E.D., I got him a job at Children's Hospital. He promised that he would not repeat KB's mistake and put me in the position of having to explain his misconduct. He kept his promise. I heard nothing but good things about David from his supervisor. In fact, he was one of her favorite employees. Everything seemed to be going well until the night KB and David took Gloria's car without permission. To make matters worse, KB was driving without a license. I resented having to wake Gloria to go to the police station because of my brothers' irresponsibility. Fortunately for them, they got off with little more than an insignificant punishment.

David started dating a woman whom I was less than thrilled about. She was nearly forty years old and had five kids! David was only eighteen. In addition, he refused to follow the rules of the house, so I asked him to leave. That's when he moved in with his forty-year-old girlfriend. Soon thereafter, he was terminated from Children's Hospital.

The following day, KB took Gloria's car without asking again, and this time he hit a drunk pedestrian. I was terrified that we were going to lose everything we had but, fortunately, no lawsuit was filed against us. Clearly, it was time for KB to leave—this time for good. I gave KB a bus ticket back to North Carolina. He had been in North Carolina only a short time when he was involved in an altercation, was stabbed multiple times, and was left for dead. He survived his injuries, but since that day, I've been on pins and needles ever, worrying that a call will come giving me the worst news imaginable. It became clear to me that I had nothing else to offer him.

As grown men, we are responsible for our lives and for the choices we make. I will not stop striving to be the best person I can be. I refuse to let pain from my past become my prison. Pain can be your poison and can kill your spirit or it can be your power to unleash your purpose. It is all about the choices you make. What you choose determines how much of life you will enjoy, how much you will accomplish, and how purposeful your life will be.

8

Change is Gonna Come

When I go to my brother and I say,
brother help me please,
my brother winds up knocking me back
down on my knees.
There's been times when I thought I
wouldn't last for long,
but now I think I'll carry on.
It's been a long time coming
but I know, a change is gonna come.

—Terence Trent D'arby

While I worked at Children's Hospital, I saw vast numbers of babies abandoned by substance-abusing parents. There was a shortage of adoptive and foster care families available for those children. As a result, the children spent the early months of their lives in hospitals. *Surely there must be something I can do*, I thought.

I decided to call one of the local nonprofit agencies, For Love of Children (FLOC). I told FLOC's foster home recruiter Valli Matthews my story about growing up in foster care and about how much I didn't want that experience for those boarder babies.

The pain and consequences of not having a permanent home are something no child should experience.

Ms. Matthews invited me to go on the Cathy Hughes morning show on WOL radio in Washington, D.C., to help recruit families. Pleased with the outcome of the radio interview, Valli then asked me to sit on a training panel for foster parents. Shortly afterward, I began receiving invitations to speak at various conferences around the country where social workers, administrators, foster families, adoptive families, and youth came together to advocate for children in need of homes. My childhood psychologist, Dr. Lewis, heard that I was coming to Albany, New York, to give a speech about my experiences in foster care and wrote to me. I still have the wonderful letter she sent.

April 30, 1993

Dear Shane—

I saw your name in the Program of "Celebrating Adoption". I would really have tried to come to hear you, but I will be out of town that week. However, I must tell you how proud I am of you, how much I admire and respect you.

Through thick & thin, ups & downs (and there were many!) I never for a moment gave up on you or stopped thinking that you were so special. It's people like you that make my work & life so rewarding.

Shane, I still have on my wall the play you wrote at 10 yrs of age called "Adopted Child". I've shown it to so many people over the years, I consider it priceless. I remember so clearly after one of your mishaps a couple of years later, your saying "I'm nobody without a family".

I think the time has come to turn it over to you — The play I mean — for you to have and show. After all, we are all family & so should Shane. I would like to hear from you — busy schedule & all — and maybe you'll honor us with a visit to NY soon!

Take care & regards to all,

Selma Lewis

I thanked her for believing in me when no one else did, and I promised that I would continue to make her proud. Dr. Lewis told me that my roommate from the Rego Park Group Home, Kenny, had asked about me, and she helped me get in touch with him. Kenny was completing graduate school in California at the time and wanted to come back East. I invited him to stay with my family and me, and he accepted.

We had a wonderful reunion, but I was shocked that, like my brother KB, Kenny felt I had abandoned him, only this time it was when I left the group home for college. I was clueless. I guess I never realized how much I meant to him, but when you're transitioning out of a group-home to adulthood, your sole focus is survival. I was seventeen and on my own. I had bigger issues than what was going on in the group home where the kids left behind had, at least, guaranteed shelter. In retrospect, I can now see what he meant, but all he had to do was write me, and I would definitely have written back. I think he still lives in the Washington, D.C. area, but we don't keep in touch—a fact that saddens me.

The speaking circuit has been a wonderful experience. I've met some fascinating people who are very committed to better outcomes for youth. I've met some wacky ones too. Many are driven more by power and turf than by the opportunity to promote healing and transformation in our communities and our children. It's always refreshing when I get the chance to be in the company of people who genuinely care about kids, people who are willing to break down whatever barriers exist to make things right.

On my way to one engagement, I had the most phenomenal reunion. As my plane landed in Seattle, I remembered hearing that Reverend Kennedy, my former dad, had relocated to Seattle and had died of a heart attack. I decided to look up his mother and sister to see how they were doing and to let them know how I was doing. I had no idea how to get in touch with them, but I remembered that he always talked about how much he had loved being a member of Mt. Zion Baptist Church when he was a little boy. I called Mt. Zion, explained that I had been one of Reverend Kennedy's foster children, that I had recently learned of his death, and that I wanted to know how to reach his family.

The woman on the other end of the phone said, "Reverend Kennedy isn't dead." He was alive, well, and working as a school principal. Talk about a surprise! I was so thrilled that Reverend Kennedy was okay, but I was also nervous about seeing him after all we'd gone through. With my friend Jackie providing moral support, I decided to pay a visit to Reverend Kennedy's school.

When he emerged from his office, he was surprised to see me. He embraced me warmly and seemed genuinely pleased to see me. We spoke briefly, and I invited him to come hear me speak. He couldn't commit but he said he would try to make it. I said good bye to Reverend Kennedy, not knowing if I'd ever see him again, but it sure felt good to let him see that I'd made it and that I was doing fine.

Just as I began my speech at the "One-Church-One-Child" conference, Reverend Kennedy strolled into the hotel ballroom. I was startled at first but remained focused on my remarks. As I acknowledged him from the podium, it dawned on me that many of the rules he imposed on me—that I rebelled against—were the same rules I was imposing on Tiffany. I acknowledged in my remarks that I wasn't able to receive the love he was trying to give me when I was in his home. Knowing how much I still desired a relationship with a father, I asked him, "Is it too late for me to ask you to be my dad?"

"No, it's not," he said, and in that moment we connected.

This personal reunion and speech had a far greater than expected effect on some members of the audience. One minister declared that he was going to go searching for his long lost son. Father Clement committed to strengthening his relationship with his son, Joey. Many fathers decided to reunite or to have better relationships with their children. How powerful! What a wonderful sense of purpose that experience gave me.

Shortly after my return from Seattle, I received a late-night call from my grandmother. My Aunt Cookie (Sylvia) was found dead outside a four-story building in Harlem. Her death was treated as a homicide at first, but then authorities concluded that she might have jumped. I don't know if we'll ever know for sure. I told

Grandma that I would pay for Aunt Cookie's funeral, which was my way of doing for my mother's sister what I would have wanted to do for my mom. It was my opportunity for closure. At the funeral, I saw my aunt's son, Omar, for the first time in more than fourteen years. I had often asked Grandma about him, but she had refused to put us in touch.

Omar was a handful, and Grandma knew I would probably try to take on that responsibility on also. It turns that out he was living in a group home and was bitter and filled with rage. I would tell Grandma repeatedly that maybe Omar needed me because I could understand what he was going through, but Grandma insisted that I didn't need to take on anything else.

Whether Grandma liked it or not, I was determined to speak with Omar. He barely remembered me, but I remembered him well. He was the oldest of Aunt Cookie's five children, all of whom were in foster care at one point or another. At first, I just promised to stay in touch with him. Then I invited him to come back to Maryland with me so that we could get to know each other better. The folks at the group home thought coming with me had to be better than what awaited Omar back in the rough neighborhood where he lived. Omar was a tough guy, having secured a place on several "Most Wanted" neighborhood lists.

After the funeral, I returned home with Omar. With a telephone number given to him by his stepfather, he hoped to reunite with his siblings. Omar was heartbroken to discover that he had a wrong number and no clue how to contact his brothers and sisters. Thank goodness he was at my house when he realized this and not in New York by himself. There is no telling how he would have dealt with his anger if I had not been there for him.

I did not realize it when I invited him home, but I learned from his group home that Omar's last hope to turn his life around was a program called Glenn Mills in Pennsylvania. Gloria and I promised Omar that if he successfully completed Glenn Mills, he would always have a family standing beside him, and that as long as he was enrolled, we would visit him regularly. A little more than two years later with all promises kept, including regular home visits with us on weekends and holidays, Omar graduated from

Glenn Mills with his high school diploma and a G.E.D. Gloria and I were so proud of him, and we knew that once again we had been used to transform a life from pain to promise. When Omar came back to live with us after graduation, I helped him get a job at Children's Hospital, and he performed in an exemplary manner. Eventually, he left our home and got a place of his own with his girlfriend.

My relationship with my grandmother had grown, and we talked on the phone every day about everything. We initially built the relationship around developing strategies to ensure that my sister, Shanique, successfully transitioned to adulthood and did not get jacked up by some dude before she graduated from high school. That goal was enough to create a strong bond between us. It wasn't very long after Omar moved out that my grandmother become fed up with Shanique and sent her to live with Gloria and me. Unfortunately, we were not as successful with her as we had hoped to be.

While Gloria and I were at work one day, we left Shanique to baby sit Tiffany, Shane Rico, Brittney, and Courtney. When I got home from work, Shanique was nowhere to be found, and Tiffany was playing with the kitchen stove. When I confronted Shanique about her behavior, she simply shrugged her shoulders and said "So?" I went bonkers. I had flashbacks of our mother leaving me unattended. I simply lost it. That was the end of her stay. She was back in New York in less than a week's time.

I started having an increasing desire to be closer to my grandmother. In my early thirties by now, the more I fought the desire, the stronger it became. I finally just gave in and acknowledged the need. At that point, I really began to enjoy and appreciate our relationship for everything it had become, rather than grieving for all that it had not been. We became best friends. Over time, each telephone conversation ended with my asking her when she was going to leave New York and come spend some time with me. Each time she'd give me the same answer, "Oh, it won't be long." One day, however, when I called and she gave me that usual answer, I wouldn't accept it.

I said, "Ma, all of these years, I've never needed nor asked anything from you, but I need you now. I need you to come down and be with me. Let me lie in your lap like a big baby and just hold me. I need you to get to know my kids and for them to get to know you."

Not a second passed before she responded and said, "I'll be there." She came, and I did just as I'd told her I needed to do. After a couple of days, I put my head in her lap and just lay there. She caressed my face. As I told her how tired I was, tears started to fall. "I don't know how much more of this I can do. I've been fighting all my life to survive, trying not to repeat the mistakes of my mom and dad. But every day, it seems to get harder. It's a struggle getting through. Sometimes I'm tired of carrying this burden and of feeling as if nobody understands how hard it is to be me."

She softly said, "I know, baby, I know." And I just lay there quietly. For the first time since my mom walked out on me, I was being held and touched by a parent. It was a strange sensation, and it let me know I'm human. Never again did I have to ask again; Mom's visits became steady. My home was her second home, her escape from New York.

She began to change, to soften and open up, as we spent time together. We both did. I laughed with her and teased her about her weight, and she teased me about mine. It's somewhat funny that everything I hoped to find in all those homes, I ultimately found with my grandmother, the woman who at first rejected me. I often wonder what my life would have been like if I'd just left her alone, not pursued her. I would have never experienced the beauty and strength of our relationship, and neither would my children.

9

Our Song

Your image of me is what I hope to be.
I've treated you unkindly, but you can
see,
there's no one else more important to me.
But we're alone now, and I'm singing this
song for you.
—You taught me precious secrets …
of a true love withholding nothing;
you came out in front when I was hiding.
—Now, I'm so much better.
I told you all of my secrets,
because no one else seemed to care.
Never forget when we were alone,
I sang this song for you.

—A. Nesby

Watching my grandmother and my children interact felt great, although at times it felt unbelievable to the point of fantasy. Grandma didn't miss anything. I don't know why, but something inside me warmed up when I heard her scold them. Perhaps it was the knowledge that my wife had someone she could consistently rely on for relief from all the kids. Maybe it was hearing my children call her "grandma" and knowing that they were experiencing what I never had. Whatever it was, it made me feel as if I belonged somewhere, even if I got there through my children.

It's amazing, but when you work hard at forgiving, letting go, and living in the present, trouble really doesn't have to last always. The love I wasn't able to get from a family as a child, I got as a man through my children, wife, and grandmother.

At times, Grandma and I were inseparable, and then at times, when my moods kicked in, I felt claustrophobic—as if I were suffocating. Those moments passed quickly, though. One thing was for sure: Shane loved his Grandma, and Grandma sure loved her grandson Shane.

Given our history, not many people understand how our relationship evolved into something this great. Some immediate and extended family members even resented that I dropped everything when she called, and every need she had—that I was aware of—was attended to. You could say, "time heals wounds," but that would be too trite. I prefer the Covey principle, "Seek first to understand, before seeking to be understood." I try to live by that principle in all that I do. When I have turned away from something or someone, it is either because I have exhausted my capacity for understanding or because I found malice in the heart of the person or in that person's intent.

I got to know my grandmother after I graduated from high school, and our growing relationship has allowed her to be honest about her feelings and the choices she made before and after my birth. The stories she told me about that time have helped me not only to understand and respect her, but, also, to realize whom I am. Her revelations also equipped me to make it impossible to let others define me ever again. As I recount some of what she shared with me, perhaps you too will understand how multigenerational pain contributed to the abandonment of my brother and me and to understand what fueled my determination to break that cycle with my children, my siblings, and my cousins. Perhaps there's someone in your life you can try to understand better so your own cycle of healing can begin.

♦   ♦   ♦

You see, Sherry's grandmother Flossy was a New York City showgirl. It was her goal-driven, succeed-at-any-cost attitude that made her walk away from her infant daughter and husband to further her showgirl career, providing entertainment for the merchant marines. On a blustery winter day, Flossy wrapped little Sandra warmly in a blanket and left the child on the doorstep of her Aunt Gertie. Flossy walked away and never looked back. Gertie was shocked that Flossy would do such a thing, but she was happy to have Sandra to rear as her own.

Sandra, my grandmother, grew up following her mother's colorful career, but Flossy showed no interest in her. In fact, she appeared to go out of her way to act is if Sandra had never been born. It shattered Sandra's heart to think that the woman who gave birth to her could deny her. Aunt Gertie did her best to counteract the damage Flossy's rejection had done. As often as possible, she reassured Sandra that she was beautiful and told her repeatedly that she could be anything she wanted to be. Aunt Gertie told Sandra that she could even be a showgirl, just like her mother, if she wanted. "I'll be anything but like my mother," Sandra insisted.

The years of abandonment and neglect changed Sandra's feelings for her mother from disappointment to hatred. However, she adored her Aunt Gertie, and Sandra was devastated when Gertie suddenly died. Sandra was just eighteen, and the only mother she had ever known was gone. She was alone, scared, and broke; she had no marketable skills other than the domestic abilities she had acquired at home. In her vulnerable state, the first man who came along—Leroy, a high yellow brother with freckles—had no trouble charming the stockings off her. Their marriage didn't last, however, because Leroy was abusive to Sandra from the start.

When Sandra returned home from the hospital after having their first child, Leroy raped her, rupturing her so terribly she had to be rushed back to the hospital. The doctors and nurses couldn't believe the damage Leroy's attack had done.

Sandra eventually left Leroy and moved to New Jersey, but it wasn't long before she took Leroy back and allowed him and his mother to move in with her. That turned out to be the worst mistake of her life. Leroy drank excessively and beat her up regularly. She didn't know which was more painful—getting her ass beaten or the humiliation of Leroy's mother looking on with approval.

"A man's got to do what a man's got to do," his mother would say. Sandra always knew that Leroy's mother felt that she wasn't good enough for him, and finally Sandra had come to the conclusion that her mother-in-law was right. She didn't deserve Leroy, and she didn't deserve to be abused. However, Sandra didn't think she could do much better than Leroy, so she tried to make the marriage work. Mostly, she stayed because she didn't want to abandon her child the way her mother, Flossy, had abandoned her.

Confused and conflicted, Sandra had another child with Leroy. She left him again, but he found out where she was living, kicked in the door, and carried her and the two children back to New Jersey where they sold bootleg liquor for a living. Their third child (my mother, Sherry) was born shortly thereafter.

Sandra, Leroy, and their three children eventually moved to Hartford, Connecticut. During an argument, Leroy threw his wife out of a moving car, and she rolled down into a ditch. A passerby saved her life by calling an ambulance. The only good thing about that incident was that Leroy never found her again. Sandra didn't know if Leroy never tried to locate her because he thought she was dead, or if he was afraid she would call the police. Whatever the reason, she was at last free of Leroy.

Sandra met a new love, and although it didn't last, she had her fourth child with him. She became an erotic dancer to feed her children. While dancing in nightclubs, she met a sailor named Eric and had her fifth and sixth children with him. Eventually, Sandra got her own place in the South Bronx.

Although she was a single mother of six now, Sandra still thought she was a little hot thing. Her new boyfriend, Vernon, must have thought likewise, because he would think nothing of jumping on the subway on the Upper West Side, where he lived, and traveling to the South Bronx for an occasional booty call. By then, Sandra didn't take stuff from anyone, especially when it came to protecting her kids. It was not unusual to see Sandra in the street fighting someone who had messed over one of her babies. Life had taught her that families stick together, and that they defend each other no matter what. She made sure all the kids remembered that fact every day before they walked out the door.

It was no secret that Sandra's boys were her favorites. Her sons could do no wrong. However, when it came to her daughter, Sherry, she was particularly protective. I guess you have to be when your daughter is one of the prettiest girls in the neighborhood and, at thirteen, one of the last remaining virgins. Every little roughneck on the block had staked his claim to Sherry. At thirteen years old, Sherry was arrested for stealing, but Sandra was certain that Sherry was set up, never for one minute doubting her innocence.

The detective was hauling Sherry off in handcuffs when he accidentally hit her in the eye. Instinctively and with no regard for the fact that the officer was carrying a gun, Sandra picked up the closest frying pan and hit him on his head. All hell broke loose. In the end, both mother and daughter were handcuffed and taken to the police station. The judge released Sandra, but sent Sherry away for a year to Hudson Juvenile Home for Girls.

After Sherry was released from Hudson, Sandra really tightened the reins on her, refusing to let Sherry out of her sight. Boyfriends were out of the question for Sherry until Sandra's boyfriend Vernon suggested that he introduce Sherry to his little brother David. With Sherry always in the house, Vernon couldn't get enough "private time" with her mother. David could keep Sherry busy while Vernon got busy with Sandra. At first, Sandra wasn't too keen on the idea. "I ain't having any stuff in my house," Sandra warned.

"You don't have a thing to worry about," Vernon assured her. "Dee Dee ain't nothing to worry about, and you know I'll jack him up if he tries anything. Besides, it's time for Sherry to have a little freedom; you can't keep that girl locked up like that."

Eventually, Vernon got his way, and Sandra allowed Dee Dee to come around with Vernon and keep company with Sherry. Dee Dee turned on the charm and hit it off with Sandra immediately. His gift of gab gave her the impression that he was a good kid. The truth of the matter was that sixteen-year-old Dee Dee was nothing but a smooth-talking, dope-dealing hustler and a master thief. In his short life, he had already spent as much time in juvenile detention as he had spent at home. Sherry found his charm irresistible, and none of the other boys in the neighborhood stood a chance after that.

When Dee Dee discovered that Sherry was not only beautiful but could sing too, he melted like butter. It wasn't long after she met Dee Dee that Sherry fell in love, surrendered her virginity, and become pregnant with me. It all happened with Vernon and Sandra locked in the next room, too busy with each other to realize I was being conceived on the living room couch.

Sherry was terrified of her mother's response when she found out she was pregnant. She knew that Sandra had big dreams for her daughter. The thought of Sherry repeating her mother's mistakes was unacceptable. Sherry couldn't stop thinking about all the times her mother had warned her not to get pregnant and what Sandra threatened to do if any daughter of hers dared to disobey.

"You better not bring any babies up in here. If any of you come in here pregnant, I'm telling you, I'll beat it out of you."

If there was one thing Sherry knew about her mother, it was that she said what she meant and meant what she said. She had to keep her pregnancy a secret from her mother for her own safety and the safety of her baby.

A neighbor finally gave away Sherry's secret. She commented to Sandra that Sherry seemed to be getting a bit big and asked, "Girl, you sure she ain't pregnant?"

"Hell no! I don't let Sherry out of my sight," Sandra insisted. "Besides, she knows I'd beat her ass down if she tried to come in here with a baby."

But later that evening, as soon as Sherry walked in the door, Sandra made Sherry take off her clothes, and there was no doubt that Sherry was very pregnant. The sight of Sherry's bulging tummy sent Sandra into a hysterical rage. She started pounding on Sherry with her fists and screaming at the top of her lungs, "I'm gonna beat you till it drops out of you."

Sherry fell to the floor and curled herself into a knot, trying desperately to protect her child from her mother's punches, kicks, and stomps, crying and begging her to stop. It seemed the beating was never going to end until finally, exhausted and out of breath, Sandra stopped. The terrible abuse was surely enough to cause Sherry to miscarry, but amazingly, both my mother and I made it through. I had won my very first fight for survival.

Having failed in her attempt to beat the baby out of her daughter, Sandra plotted to have Sherry's pregnancy terminated. "...You are not bringing no baby in here; we are getting rid of it," she told her daughter. Sandra made an appointment and dragged Sherry to an illegal, backdoor abortion house. They had only just begun prepping her for the procedure, when Sherry jumped off the table, grabbed her clothes, and bolted out of the door.

"You are not going to kill my baby," she screamed and left the abortion house, putting on her clothes as she ran. Sandra eventually had to accept the fact that Sherry was determined to keep her baby and that I was going to be born.

Things didn't look good at all when the time came for Sherry to deliver. She was just fifteen years old, with blood pressure so high the doctors didn't think she would survive the birth, although they thought they could save the baby. A priest was called to perform last rites. Sandra nearly collapsed when she heard this. She couldn't believe her daughter was near death giving birth to a child Sandra didn't approve of or welcome. Sandra went to the chapel and prayed for Sherry's life. "God, if you have to take one of them, please take this baby and let Sherry live," she pleaded. And God did what she asked, and more.

Sherry miraculously survived the life-threatening complications, and on November 21, 1963, at 11:20 p.m., I was born as David Earl Williams, Jr. weighing in at 7 pounds 11 ounces. My name was changed from David to Shane, thanks to Grandma. Sandra hated my father so much that she told the hospital records clerk that she would "kick her ass" if David Williams showed up on that birth certificate. Wisely, the terrified clerk chose not to risk a confrontation and issued my birth certificate with the name Shane Lenard Salter, per my grandmother's instructions. The choice of Shane was inspired by the old western movie starring Allan Ladd, and Lenard was to honor my uncle, John Lenard. Shane, a variation of John, means God's most gracious gift in Greek. In Hebrew, it means "beautiful". Salter is my grandmother's last name. The first Mr. Salter was a white Englishman from a family of salt miners, who married a freed slave when he settled in the United States.

A few years after I was born, my mother applied for public assistance, and we moved to our own apartment in the basement of a brownstone in Harlem. It was my father, Dee Dee, who introduced my mother to drugs, which eventually led to her heroin addiction. With Dee Dee in and out of jail, my mother met Norman, a much older man, who tried unsuccessfully to help her get off drugs. Norman fathered my mother's second son, KB, who was born in 1966.

Of course, I knew none of this story while growing up. All I knew was that my family wasn't there. I didn't understand for many years what had happened to my mother or why she didn't come back for us. Now I know and I understand. While I don't excuse or justify my mother's actions, I certainly understand her pain, and I understand how this happened in spite of her best intentions.

I have learned from the pain in my grandmother's eyes that, because she was abandoned as an infant, she couldn't give my mother what she needed. She wanted to break the cycle. She did the best with what she had, and it just wasn't enough. That's why it's so crucial that all children get from us what we know they will need to give to their children someday. Love them, and they will know how to love and give love. Encourage them, and they will know how to encourage and give encouragement. See the best in them, and they will see the best in others. Tell them they are beautiful and strong and have a purpose, and they will treat others as if they are beautiful and strong and have a purpose. Give them a safe place to call home, and they will make sure theirs is a safe place to call home. Show them that no matter how dark the moment, how powerful the enemy, "Trouble Don't Last Always," and they will be rooted in the knowledge that tomorrow is a new beginning and is worth living for.

Child abuse and neglect are largely an intergenerational problem. Although it is clear that the nature and severity of some types of abuse can be caused by mental illness or character disorders, many parents who abuse and neglect their children were abused themselves. They try to cope with environmental stresses and the demands of parenting, but they have few resources to meet those challenges and many terrible memories to cope with. When I understood this truth, that knowledge helped me both to open the door to true forgiveness, and to recognize and confront my own demons.

10

You Were Loved

You were loved by someone, touched by
someone, held by someone,
meant something to someone.
You loved somebody; you touched
somebody's heart along the way.
When it's all over ...you can look back
and say,
you did ok,
you were loved.

—W. Houston

On Christmas night 1999, I received a call from Mom Jenkins telling me that her son Robbie had died. I offered to go home to be with her and the family. I was mystified when she told me not to.

"It's the holiday; we can't do anything right now," she said. "I'll call you with the arrangements."

A few days later, she left me a voice mail, referring to herself as "Doris," which was very strange. She was always "Mom" to Grandma, my children, and me—never "Doris." I attributed her behavior to stress. She asked me to write Robbie's obituary, and I immediately agreed, excited that she wanted me to perform such an important task, to know that I was valued and still fitted in. I went to work on it right away. I was so proud of what I wrote and was eager to show it to her. I was surprised when she became irritated that my first draft stated that Robbie had died "after a long illness."

"Take that out," she snapped.

I was puzzled. It had been a long illness. But I put my feelings aside. After all, he was *her* son, and maybe I wasn't supposed to be grieving because he was not my natural brother.

During the funeral when I placed a hand on her back to comfort her, she whispered, "Don't touch me." At that point, I knew she was angry with me, but why?

On the way back from the cemetery after Robbie's burial, I asked Mom Jenkins if I could have a small token from Robbie's apartment as a keepsake. She snapped at me again, saying, "He didn't have anything; I don't know what you want."

At that point, I decided it was best not to say anything more to her. I thought I understood the depth of her pain, because I too was in pain. But it seemed much more than that. Could it be that the mother who raised me was angry because it was Robbie who was dead—instead of me? If not, it sure felt like it. I was not supposed to be the one who survived. I was not supposed to be the one who completed college. But they had helped to make all that possible. I knew that I wouldn't have survived without them. Mom and Dad

Jenkins meant the world to me, and I thought I meant just as much to them. I never missed an opportunity to show the depth of my gratitude.

But it seems that I was stuck in time. Everything and everyone moved on after KB and I left, except me. KB wanted to stay. I didn't agree with him and never understood why he wouldn't keep in touch with any of the families or Grandma. Whenever we left a home and said good bye, KB meant good bye and didn't look back. If you sent him packing, he would accept that finality.

I just didn't see things that way as a child. To me, they were still my parents, but to them, the day KB and I were sent off to the failed adoption, I became nothing more than their former foster child. How could that be? All those years of treating me like a son—Catholic schools, reconstructive dental work and so forth. The Jenkins family was the most stable force throughout my life. I always stayed in contact with them, giving periodic updates on my progress and accomplishments. Was I living a fantasy to keep myself safe? Was this one of my efforts to latch onto somebody else's family to help with my transition to adulthood? Were the accomplishments I shared with them over the years—as would any normal child—adding insult to injury because Robbie was struggling? Was I supposed to be out of their lives? I simply thought they would be proud of the return on their investment, and I wanted to hear someone who knew me as a little boy say, "I'm proud of you, son."

I think one of the reasons I went into healthcare was that I wanted Ma Jenkins to feel she had influenced me because she was a registered nurse. If there was any place I thought I had identity, any place where I could be myself and get love and acceptance, it was with the Jenkinses. What happened at the funeral was so painful that I couldn't face it. I couldn't talk about it for a long time. I dealt with it in therapy, but it's probably still inside me somewhere.

Ma Jenkins and I didn't speak at all until five years later when I happened to run into her at a wedding of a friend in Washington, D.C. It was ironic that she and I knew the same people. I could never have imagined she would be there. I became very nervous, wondering how she would react to me this time. After some folks in the family encouraged us, we posed together for a couple of pictures. I gave her a hug, looked her dead in the eye and told her what I felt in my soul, finishing with "No matter what, I still love you and there's nothing you can do about it."

I don't know if she was embarrassed, overwhelmed, or what, but her only response was "You're squishing my glasses."

I later learned that after Robbie's death, Dad Jenkins took seriously ill, which, sadly, meant that Mom Jenkins was spending all of her retirement caring for people she loved who were gravely ill: first her son and then her husband.

I finally worked up the nerve to call her, and we actually had a good conversation about everything—except the reason we didn't talk for all those years. We never got quite back to our old relationship, but I thought the healing process had begun until several years later on a late Friday afternoon before the Labor Day weekend.

On that day, I received a phone call at my office in Washington, DC. It felt like deja vu. "Shane, this is Doris."

"Hi mom," I replied. Without pause she said, "Bob died last Sunday."

Because I could not allow her to diminish who he was to me, I asked, "You mean Dad?"

"Yeah," she answered.

"I couldn't find your telephone number, Shane," she continued. "Sorry I couldn't reach you earlier, but the wake is this Saturday and the Mass will be on Labor Day."

My thoughts started racing. It took her five days to call me? Why? It seemed twisted, but she appeared to have no regard for the effect that the death of the one man who, undoubtedly, always believed in and understood me, would have on me. Did she just block out all those years or forget that I am the same person as the child they both helped raise? Although all grown-up now, I am more grateful and loyal than the universe has words to capture.

"I will be there, Mom," I told her. I hung up the phone and let the tears flow before calling a good friend and sobbing uncontrollably. Afterwards, I regained my composure and left for what would be the most painful Labor Day weekend of my life.

I thought I was prepared for anything, but not the heartache of being told that I had to ride in a van behind the family limousine because there was no room left in the car. Beaten, bruised, maybe covered with scars too deep to camouflage, I still remained determined to comport myself with grace and dignity, determined to respect her grief and anger. Even though I am an adult now, I continue to see Mom and Dad Jenkins through my eyes as a child who sought and was given a safe harbor. She is my mother, and he will always be my daddy.

Dad Jenkins's burial service with honors

There is one thing that is great about being an adult—you don't have to keep begging for unconditional love and acceptance; you don't have to keep calling and visiting all the time as I had to do when I was a kid in order to keep a roof over my head. I am learning to love and to accept myself unconditionally, which is good enough for now.

I just don't have the motivation to be the driver in relationships anymore. I noticed over the years that if I didn't initiate contact, most of my relationships eventually dwindled away. Well lately, I've just let this one and a lot of others die.

There is one relationship, however, that no matter how much I wanted to, I just couldn't abandon. For a while after I ran away from my father, I was too afraid to visit him. While I was attending Elmira College, I heard that he had been stabbed nine times and had almost lost his life. But even then, I didn't try to get in touch; I was just too uncomfortable around him. Finally, one summer when I returned from school, I decided to visit him. That was the day he drove me by an abandoned building in the Bronx. It was no ordinary place. "The bodies of the men who tried to kill me are in that building," he boasted, pointing at a dilapidated garden apartment.

I knew about some of his other crimes. But a murderer? It was beyond belief. *I am the son of a murderer*, I kept telling myself.

Over the years, his progressive deterioration made me sad, but I had no respect left for him. After my first daughter, Tiffany, was born, I refused to call him Dad and started calling him by his street name, Dee Dee. Now that I was a father with my own vision of what a father should be, I couldn't bring myself to call him Dad anymore. Still, as I matured and grew spiritually, I found myself compelled to follow the command: "Honor thy Father and thy Mother." I recognized that we are commanded to honor our parents even if they fail to measure up to our expectations. I also realized that at the end of my own earthly journey, I wouldn't be judged by what kind of father I had, but by what kind of son I was. After that revelation our relationship, improved significantly. But the truth is that when my father died, even though by then I could love him, I felt relieved. At the time of his death, his youngest child was two years old. I could only pray that no more of my family members would enter the foster care system or become addicted to drugs.

I always knew I would be responsible for his funeral arrangements, and although finances were very tight in my house at the time, I did my duty. None of his siblings or family members would contribute to the expenses for one reason or another. To cut costs, I asked a friend who was an ordained minister to ride with me from Washington, D.C., and to preside at his service. When she asked me what she should know about him, I told her the truth. My father had been a thief, drug dealer, drug addict, and self-described murderer—not exactly a model father. I insisted that her eulogy be honest. His sister agreed to dress him in a short-sleeved golf shirt, pants, and tennis shoes, the same outfit that he wore every day. He never looked more peaceful or better—no gray hairs and skin smooth as silk.

At the service, the minister, Reverend Lassiter, did an awesome job. She kept it real, just as I had asked her. It was the right choice. Everyone appreciated and recognized the person we were talking about and the soul we were praying for. If there is such a thing as a good funeral, this was one.

But there was no disguising the facts of my background. And that's why my great-grandmother begged me to live my life, to leave my family alone, and to never look back. She thought that this estranged family of mine was only going to bring me down. However, I am who I am, and it's not in my nature to turn my back on folks whom I care about. So I didn't follow her advice and continued to pursue relationships with as many members of my family as I could find.

When my great-grandmother died, sadly, she had lost most of her material wealth. As she had become less mobile, she had entrusted her possessions to a "friend"—a friend who robbed her blind. Even the baby grand piano was gone.

It was equally painful to watch my great-granddad slip away. Toward the end of his life, he developed Alzheimer's. As a result, he wasn't able to recognize me when I visited him in the hospital.

He was the only one who made me believe I was remembered while in foster care, and now he didn't know me anymore. That was hard. But I had memories to fall back on: every time I looked at that old baby shoe, I would remember how he had thought about me and believed in me when that mattered the most. I made peace with his condition, realizing that it could not affect our relationship, and I accepted that my great-granddad was leaving us one day at a time. It was not long before he peacefully closed those bright eyes for the last time and left on his final journey.

11

Still I Rise

Shaken but here I stand, weary still I press on.
Long are the nights, the tears I cry.
Dark are the days, no sun in the sky.
Yet still I rise, never to give up,
never to give in.
Against all odds, yet still I rise higher than the clouds.
Sometimes I'm troubled but not in despair,
although struggling,
I make my way through.
Trials they come to make me strong,
I must endure; I must hold on.

—Yolanda Adams

Great-granddad's vision of my life as transforming and redeeming is the greatness I believe we can all achieve and are called to achieve. After leaving Children's Hospital (my first job after the Navy), I began a professional career in child welfare and served as the Chief Operating Officer of For Love of Children (FLOC). FLOC was one of the largest family support nonprofits in Washington, D.C. This position was an opportunity for me to develop patience, to confront the realities of how the system really worked, and to see the worst and best in people—all in the name of serving children.

Life came full circle. I was no longer the kid upset because as soon as he started college, his group-home bed was assigned to someone else. Now, as a child welfare administrator, I was the person who gave that bed away. I was presiding over a system that asked me to "ensure maximum census for full reimbursement." In other words, many of my decisions were driven by how we could meet payroll, not what was best for the kids. I was also disheartened by my agency's inability to offer additional services to the number of children seeking support after being discharged from our program. Is it any wonder that 45 percent of those leaving foster care become homeless within a year?

The CEO and I were as different as day and night, but we complimented each other. He was an incredible visionary from Kentucky, and I was an urban cowboy from the South Bronx. Fred was a passionate, no-frills advocate for children, and I learned a great deal while working with him.

After my tenure with FLOC, I served as the national director of the Marriott Foundation for People with Disabilities. That job was my introduction to corporate America. What a challenge it was transitioning from a nonprofit, where the prevailing sentiment was "Can't we all just get along?" to Marriott, where I was regularly reminded that, it didn't matter that we were a nonprofit organization, our service had to be run like an efficient business— just like every other subsidiary of the Marriott Corporation.

Shortly after arriving, the CEO took me to meet Richard Marriott and introduced me as the new national director. I shook Mr. Marriott's hand and gave him a hug. I hug everybody and never thought anything of it. Apparently, this was not the Marriott culture. Pulling me aside, my CEO told me, "You should get to know people before you hug them."

I was mortified. My second day on the job, and I had already managed to ruin my career. For weeks, I replayed that scenario in my head, thinking what a fool I had made of myself until, one day, I was told that the CEO had apologized for me the next time he saw Mr. Marriott, explaining that I had just come from the nonprofit community. "That Shane is quite a hugger isn't he?" he said to Mr. Marriott.

I'm sure he was surprised to hear Mr. Marriott reply, "Yes, and we sure could use a lot more hugging around here." My experience at Marriott turned out to be wonderful, and by the time I left, we were a "hugging" foundation.

I then became the director of the Freddie Mac Foundation. The absolute, greatest outcome of that experience was the expansion of my family. One Sunday morning, I was watching the repeat of WRC's "Wednesday's Child," featuring two brothers in need of a family. Moyé and Nigel were three and five years old at the time and reminded me of KB and me. I instantly fell in love with them. Not only were they adorable, but also here was an opportunity to keep two little brothers together. Hard though I tried, I couldn't put them out of my mind. I spoke to "Saint" Gloria, making the case that our influence could help those two boys grow into healthy, productive young men. Besides, Tiffany was going to graduate from high school in June, my son David had already graduated and moved into his own apartment, and Shane Rico was away. The only children left in our house were Brittney and Courtney. Although our home had seemed just the right size when we had purchased it, it now felt very large. Surely, there was room for two more. Whenever I think back to those times, I can't help but laugh at myself. Who did I think I was? Mr. Josephine Baker?

Tiffany had become angry with me when we moved from our home in Chantilly, Virginia, to a house in Ashburn, Virginia, because it had a mother-in-law suite for my grandmother when she became too old to live alone. That move had meant Tiffany had to attend a different high school for her senior year. I totally minimized her predicament because, except when I was with the Jenkins family, I changed schools many times during my childhood. Tiffany initially said she didn't mind. Perhaps if I had stayed at one school as a teenager I'd have instinctively known that she really didn't mean that and was putting her own needs aside in favor of mine. It was touch and go there for a while—she struggled her entire senior year—but she made it. Her graduation that June meant more to me then she could imagine. Not only was she officially launched, but she was the second generation of our family with a high school diploma. I also felt a tremendous sense of achievement because I had kept the promise I had made to her at birth. I had never walked out on her and had been there from her infancy to her graduation. It wasn't always easy, but with our guardian angel, Gloria, by our side, we made it.

My daughter never knew the kind of rejection and loneliness I had known, and she hadn't joined that 22 percent of teenager girls who become pregnant. Thus, we'd broken yet another generational curse. Our relationship had its difficulties, but Tiffany decided to follow in my footsteps and enlisted in the Navy after graduation. Two months later, Gloria also completed her life goal and earned her master of science degree in Information Technology from The American University. She worked fulltime at AT&T, attended graduate school full-time, and remained focused with a house full of children. How amazing and brilliant this woman is! I keep praying that the children will model her character, discipline, and brains.

Soon after Gloria's graduation, our two new sons arrived. I was so gung ho about being a new dad that I took a couple of weeks of paternity leave. For me, two weeks off from work was unprecedented. It was like an extra Christmas, and the twinkle in Moyé and Nigel's eyes said it all. Looking at my beautiful family reminded me of how much I had overcome in my life and of how fortunate I was to have found a way out of the despair I had known.

Later in my tenure at the Freddie Mac Foundation, I was extremely pleased to be able to channel funds from the foundation to New York's Administration for Children Services (ACS), the same foster care system that had taken care of me. Formerly known as the Bureau of Child Welfare, ACS was under the leadership of Nicolas Scopetta and William Bell at the time, and I developed a good relationship with both of them. Nick was also a product of the foster care system, and I was happy that someone who had experienced foster care firsthand was leading the system in New York.

Through my friendships at ACS, I also developed a relationship with Mayor Rudi Giuliani. New York City had made a number of important reforms in foster care during his tenure, and I was able to convince the Freddie Mac Foundation to honor the mayor for his work on behalf of New York's foster children. Can you imagine what I felt when a *New York Post* editorial on December 13, 2000, reported that "An independent blue-ribbon panel is calling the Giuliani administration's effort to combat child abuse and neglect remarkable. After two years of study, the panel recently released a comprehensive good news report.... The results are clear: Real changes are possible at city agencies. Congratulations to all concerned. Your hard work has paid off."

On February 3, 2005, I read in the *Post* that "2,200 children, or more than 10 percent of all those in foster care, will be transferred to agencies with the best track records in the city's annual performance review. The poorly rated agencies had serious shortcomings in such areas as record keeping, child safety, and monitoring the care of children placed with foster parents." When I was coming through the system, we would merely have been stuck in the poor-performing agency.

I encouraged the CEO of Freddie Mac and the CEO of the Foundation to host a grand reception in the mayor's honor at Battery Park and to present the mayor with an award. I had the pleasure of presenting that award and of introducing Mayor Giuliani, and I did so with tremendous enthusiasm. This ceremony was personal. My life's work culminated right there in that room in the park. I was able to go back home to New York City and to acknowledge the mayor of my city for leading one of the largest system reform efforts ever in child welfare.

During his acceptance speech, the mayor said to the crowd, "I think Shane Salter should run for mayor," and the crowd responded with thunderous applause. I relished that moment, but at the same time, I was aware that my boss at the Foundation didn't like her subordinates getting an ounce more attention than she got, especially when *her* boss, the CEO of Freddie Mac, was present. I assured the audience that I was flattered but had no plans to leave Freddie Mac any time soon. The mayor invited me back to New York a few weeks later for lunch with him, and we sat and talked in his office for more than two and a half hours. We exchanged philosophies on leadership and management, talking deeply about our challenges and successes. While I was there, I wanted someone to pinch me.

How did I go from being a foster child in New York whom everyone rejected to sitting and enjoying casual conversation and lunch with the mayor of New York? *If my friends could see me now!* Nick Scopetta whispered afterwards, "Those of us in the cabinet don't even get that much uninterrupted time with him; he really enjoyed talking with you." The whole experience is amazing to me now, especially because September 11 was just a few months away, and Mayor Giuliani's life would be transformed once again.

Soon thereafter, the White House asked me to join President George W. Bush for the signing of the Safe and Stable Family Act. Returning to my office following the signing ceremony, I was informed by my boss that I had been terminated, effective that day, and without severance pay. I could not believe it.

How painfully ironic, I thought, to be witnessing the signing of the Safe and Stable Families Act that morning, only to have my family totally destabilized that afternoon.

Honoraria from speaking engagements were not lucrative and consistent enough to support my family, which had been enlarged by two new sons whom I desperately wanted to keep but whom I was no longer sure I could afford. All of this was circling in my head as I tried to figure out how to keep the news from my family at least for one day, so we could celebrate Grandma's birthday. I knew it was going to be hard, but I didn't realize how hard until my doorbell rang in mid-afternoon, and I opened the door to find my office belongings being delivered in cardboard boxes. That act really hit me. My mind flashed back to all those times I had been thrown out of homes as a child. Dropping to my knees, I returned to the Rock that is greater than I am.

I prayed, and through my prayers God reminded me that everything I have, He gave to me. He had placed me in those circumstances now to learn and to grow. My healing began when I acknowledged my pain and recognized that I couldn't control my life. That was Someone Else's job.

On my knees, I was reminded to remain steadfast, for no one can take from you that which is not theirs to give in the first place. I regained my determination to pick myself up and keep trying. I knew "My Change [Was] Gonna Come" if I would just be patient and endure the pruning process because "Trouble Don't Last Always." I've been rooted in both of those songs for most of my life now and strengthened, as I hope you will be, through the power of the poem "If," authored by Rudyard Kipling, and which is one of the signature poems of Alpha Phi Alpha.

IF

If you can keep your head when all about you
Are losing theirs and blaming it on you;
If you can trust yourself when all men doubt you,
But make allowance for their doubting too:
If you can wait and not be tired by waiting,
Or being lied about, don't deal in lies,
Or being hated, don't give way to hating,
And yet don't look too good, nor talk too wise;
If you can dream—and not make dreams your
master;
If you can think—and not make thoughts your
aim,
If you can meet with Triumph and Disaster
And treat those two imposters just the same:
If you can bear to hear the truth you've spoken
Twisted by knaves to make a trap for fools,
Or watch the things you gave your life to, broken,
And stoop and build 'em up with worn-out tools;
If you can make one heap of all your winnings
And risk it on one turn of pitch-and-toss,
And lose, and start again at your beginnings
And never breathe a word about your loss:
If you can force your heart and nerve and sinew
To serve your turn long after they are gone,
And so hold on when there is nothing in you
Except the Will which says to them: "Hold on!"
If you can talk with crowds and keep your virtue,
Or walk with Kings—nor lose the common touch,
If neither foes nor loving friends can hurt you,
If all men count with you, but none too much:
If you can fill the unforgiving minute
With sixty seconds' worth of distance run,
Yours is the Earth and everything that's in it,
And—which is more—you'll be a Man, my son!

While it was tough going through that kind of rejection, humiliation, and threat to my family's livelihood at the Freddie Mac Foundation, it was perhaps the most transforming event in my adult life. I am not all that I hope to be, but I am certainly not who I was. This experience taught me that living a wholesome life meant learning how to treat both triumph and disaster the same. I have been strengthened and know that we have no other choice but to keep Holding On!

I once believed that the commitment of the Freddie Mac Foundation to children was unwavering. Nothing that was done to me can change my appreciation for the fact that the Freddie Mac Foundation has made substantial contributions in many ways to children, youth, and families—both before and during the tenure of my former boss.

You can't imagine how vindicating it was when—several years after my leaving the Foundation—an extensive article was published in the *Washington Post*, capturing the essence of an external agency's investigation into allegations that the CEO of the Foundation subjected staff members to unfair employment practices. The allegations reported in the newspaper mirrored the confidential complaints I had shared with the human resources department, and which they subsequently leaked to my then boss, the day before I was unjustly fired. I couldn't help but feel sad for those remaining in that environment. I hope the atmosphere has improved and has since become a safe, healthy place for people to serve children without the threat of misplaced egos or vendettas.

I take great comfort and pride in some of the Freddie Mac Foundation's accomplishments while I was its Director of Foundation Giving. Primarily, we gave support during its formative stages to the Congressional Coalition on Adoption, co-chaired by Senators Mary Landrieu (D/LA) and Larry Craig (R/ID) at that time. Under their leadership, and with support from many others, the Coalition ultimately launched the Congressional Coalition on Adoption Institute (CCAI), a nonprofit, nonpartisan organization that is dedicated to raising awareness about the tens of thousands of foster children in this country as well as the millions of orphans around the world in need of permanent, safe, and loving homes. CCAI also attempts to eliminate the barriers that keep those children from becoming a part of a family.

The Angels in Adoption™ Program is CCAI's signature public awareness program. Every year, CCAI invites all members of Congress to select from their home state an individual, family, or organization that has significantly contributed to changing the lives of children in need through adoption and foster care. Both the "Angels" and member of Congress attend the annual Angels in Adoption™ Awards Gala, where they meet and share their personal experiences. Congressional directors of CCAI also select "National Angels," honoring recipients for their nationwide and international work. If you know of an unsung hero making a difference in the life of a child, contact the congressional representative of that district to initiate the nomination process for this distinguished award.

I am equally proud of another initiative—the support we gave to the Oliver Project through the Orphan Foundation. In 1981, the late Joseph Rivers, a former foster youth from the Syracuse area, started the Orphan Foundation of America (OFA). His goal was simple—to help orphans and foster youth as they transition from foster care to young adulthood, with particular emphasis on helping those young men and women attend college and vocational school. Twenty years later, his dream is alive and well. Through the leadership of his foster sister Eileen McCaffrey—a woman for whom I have tremendous respect who continues to passionately champion his vision—OFA truly raises national awareness of foster care issues and the comprehensive services needed for older youth nationally. I've witnessed firsthand the effect that of OFA and its scholarship partners have had on vulnerable survivors of foster care as those organizations attempt to provide a stronger safety net for foster children pursuing post-secondary education.

All I can say is, you know you are doing something right when you attract both (former) Representative Tom Delay (R/TX) and Senator Hillary Clinton (D/NY) as committed supporters. Both politicians have supported the organization and attended the Orphan Foundation's Celebration of Excellence dinner. Creating adequate services for older youth in the foster care system is an issue that requires collaboration and a nonpartisan approach. Only that spirit of cooperation and determination will help the United States realize the full potential of our children and make us the great nation we are capable of being.

In 2000, while still shell-shocked from the Freddie Mac Foundation experience, I was asked to serve as the chief of staff to the deputy mayor for Children, Youth, Families, and Elders of the District of Columbia. I consulted with William Bell, who had just become the commissioner of New York's foster care system before accepting the position. He said that, as chief of staff, I would learn more in six months than I would in many years at any other place. That comment sealed it for me.

What an awesome growth opportunity and professional challenge this was! Every day, I learned something new. One of the benchmarks of success that I set for myself was to respond to the complex and competing constituent needs so well that there would be no way that the press could use my name to embarrass Mayor Anthony Williams, himself the product of the foster care system. It certainly wasn't easy, given the agencies for which we had oversight responsibility, including the Department of Health, Child, and Family Services Administration; the Department of Human Services; the Office of Human Rights; the Office of Aging; the Department of Parks and Recreation; the State Education Office; and the Public Library System. Our agency administered the largest percentage of the city's budget, and our plates were full. It was an incredible experience and quite a roller coaster ride.

The mayor was brilliant, and like many graduates of the foster care system, was often underestimated. I related to him, admired him, felt vested in his success, and was proud to serve in an administration that was filled with incredible talent and committed to the renaissance of the nation's capital. Not even in my wildest dreams had I envisioned such a role for myself. Despite everything, I'd come a long way.

Even more rewarding, however, was serving with Deputy Mayor Carolyn Graham, who was passionate and determined to achieve gains for children in the District of Columbia. The Council for

Court Excellence found that the city's ability to reach decisions in child neglect and abuse cases and to meet the Adoption and Safe Families Act (ASFA) deadlines improved steadily, particularly in cases where children had been removed from their homes. What gave me the greatest satisfaction was the city's implementation of the Family Drug Treatment Court. If my mother had had access to a similar program, I am certain our story would have had a better outcome. Modeled after similar programs in New York, Florida, Ohio, and Virginia, the program gives mothers a chance to rebuild their lives and their families within ASFA timelines. Mothers who qualify for the program are permitted to live with their children at a treatment facility while undergoing six months of rigorous, supervised drug treatment. In addition, the women receive job training and classes in managing a household, budgeting, and parenting. At the end of that time, they enter a six-month aftercare program. One of the most significant advantages of the program is that it enables children to stay out of foster care and remain with their mothers.

Wow, what a long way we have come—in just my lifetime! Sometimes it is hard for me to believe it when I think about what was available to my family. Yet, I am acutely aware of how great the need still is. We need more treatment facilities like the one just described. Can you imagine the positive effect and overall cost savings if we invested nationwide in programs designed to ensure that families remained together? It's not only the right thing to do, but is also less of a burden on the taxpayers.

In 2002, the deputy mayor resigned, which meant that, as her chief of staff and a political appointee, I was resigning with her. I had no clue what I would do next. Then a call came from the Board of Directors at CASA (Court Appointed Special Advocates) of D.C., an organization I helped start before going to the mayor's office. Sadly, the executive director had just had a stroke. I agreed to serve as the interim executive director while I thought through my long-term options. There was no way I could say, "No." I believed in the mission of the organization and happened to be available. I did not expect to stay beyond the interim period, but once I started working there, I realized it was a perfect fit. This position was my calling. It was clear that I was supposed to return and finish what I had begun. Now, I could motivate Washingtonians to support and help find permanent homes for the 2,800 children in D.C.'s child welfare system.

I knew that CASA was one of the best-kept secret solutions for moving children through the child welfare system quickly and safely. This grassroots D.C. organization was searching for visionary leadership to engage the community in finding permanent and safe homes for abused or neglected children. Because I strongly believe that each of us holds a key to unlock the door to a child's heart, community activism was a challenge that I was prepared to accept.

My one question was determining if I could live on a nonprofit salary with seven children. Gloria and I struggled with that problem, and ultimately found a salary figure that would fit the organization's budget, yet would not have a devastating effect on our family. It was liberating to not make money the issue. Everything in my life prepared me for this opportunity to lead. I had to be true to myself by being true to others. I was truly stepping out in faith, and I have never regretted my decision. The staff, volunteers, and board of CASA for Children of D.C. have made tremendous strides. I pursue funding from every viable source so that the citizens of the Washington metropolitan area can volunteer as advocates and give children hope.

12

Why I Sing

Someone may be wondering
When I sing my song,
At times I may be crying, and nothing's
even wrong.
I sing because I'm happy,
I sing because I'm really free.
His eye is on the sparrow,
That's the reason why I sing.

—K. Franklin

To work for the government of the District of Columbia, I had to live there, so I took a tiny apartment on Capitol Hill. It turned out to be a godsend when I found that the commute of an hour to an hour and a half from Ashburn to D.C. was becoming impossible for me. Mr. Attention Deficit Disorder couldn't sit in traffic every morning and afternoon without going wild, so I moved into the District during the week and went back out to Ashburn on Friday night, returning on Monday morning.

Being by myself for a few days a week brought other changes. After running myself ragged for years and never giving myself time to think, I realized that I had to confront my pain and claim my "get out of prison" card—to look at and listen to myself so I could learn who I really was. Initially, I had thought that because I hadn't turned out too badly, the system must have been okay—with a few hiccups here and there. It wasn't until I started engaging in dialogue with my grown daughter, Tiffany, learning from my other children, and looking at the relationships I'd been unable to sustain, both personally and professionally, over the course of my life, that I realized the price I had paid for all those years of abandonment, rejection, abuse, and neglect.

As an adult, I had assured myself that I knew what love was and that I was giving it to those who mattered to me most. However, as I went through this process of self-reflection, I began to realize that I was repeating the cycle of neglect and abuse—emotionally if not physically. All my life, I'd fought to not abandon Tiffany—to not do to her what was done to me. Success meant I did not physically abandon her or walk out on her the way my parents walked out on me, but I was so *busy* providing the home and family I thought Tiffany deserved that I was an emotionally absent father. During one of our talks, she looked at me and said, in a way that wrenched my heart, "Dad, don't you realize all I ever needed was you?"

I had always tried to do the right thing. When it became clear that her birth mother was not going to step up to the plate, I got her the best mom on the planet: my wife, Gloria. I thought Tiffany should have siblings to support her through life's struggles when she grew up, so we adopted other children and had some of our own, creating a large family whose members could help each other in hard times and celebrate together in good times. Because I wanted to make sure that all the children received a good public education, I moved the family into a neighborhood in one of the best school districts in the area. But to maintain this large family in a good area, I had to take demanding jobs with long hours. Between working to assure sure that my children would not have the negative experience that I had and fulfilling my desire to change the plight of other faceless American children in foster care, I burned myself out and became emotionally bankrupt. My kids got an emotional blank check from me, even though it was signed "with love." I had the best of intentions, but my execution wasn't enough.

Somewhere along the line, everything became about the mechanics of love and not about love itself. I had received training on real intimacy and good parenting, and I understood them intellectually but, in reality, I ran from both of them. No matter how many people I had around me, I felt isolated and lonely.

I think one of the biggest challenges faced by many abused or neglected children is dealing with social and interpersonal relationships, which has certainly been my greatest challenge. As much as I love my family and as proud as I am of my life, I wish I could have learned, as a young adult, the skills that I would need later in life to create healthy intimacies and to resolve conflicts.

I am lucky that I was able to bond with my mother during the first four years of my life. Many abandoned kids (including my own brother, KB), never get the chance to bond with anyone and that lack affects them deeply. Bonding; learning to trust; learning what you truly like and dislike; learning to recognize what you want and then learning how to ask for it; learning to say no and set boundaries; learning to be yourself and to stop wearing masks all the time—these are things children must learn how to do before they can become healthy adults.

Resolving conflict is also a challenge for many abused or abandoned kids, particularly those in foster care. If your environment changes every time the going gets tough, how do you ever learn to work things out? Of course, the adults you live with have to be willing to work things out with you as well. As you can tell from reading the first part of this book, some of the adults in my life could do this, and some couldn't. And there wasn't anything I could do about that then. But I *can* do something about it now! As an adult, I can choose the people who are part of my life. In addition to developing conflict resolution skills, I have learned how to let go of people who are toxic and unwilling to love me for me. Both those abilities have made a big difference in my life.

Because I had to depend on myself when I was young, I didn't know how to depend on others. I gave and gave. Neither did I know how to receive and would, therefore, wallow in disappointment when my needs weren't met. I was caught in a vicious circle—unable to let people give me what I needed, unable to feel that I ever fitted in. Being with people became more and more of a burden.

When I was younger, I never asked myself what *I* wanted, what *I* needed, or what was right for *me*. First, I focused on what my foster parents wanted, and later I focused on making sure that Tiffany and the rest of my family had what they wanted. I thought happiness rested on pleasing others and on meeting or exceeding expectations. Because of that belief, after Tiffany graduated, joined the Navy, and was on her own, I felt the expectations that I had set for myself when she was born had been met. I began falling apart—almost like a mother with empty nest syndrome, except my nest wasn't empty! My nest still had plenty of children in it and a beautiful wife whom I was not treating as a partner. I had been consumed by being a patriarch, and I had nothing left. I couldn't be a lover, a husband, a father, or even just plain Shane. I didn't have any of the skills I needed to be a real person—without the masks and the roles and the demands that had filled my life. Those facades were my life.

The idea of being totally alone in a room was terrifying, but I realized that solitude was what I needed to enable me to discover and embrace myself. So I moved into my D.C. apartment fulltime. Although we continued to function as a family, I did not live with Gloria and the children for several years. I chose for the first time in my life to live alone and face my demons. I struggled to work through my stuff with hopes of becoming the best man I could be, but only now, in my forties, am I learning who I really am, how to love myself, and how to let other people love me as well. My family and I now are living together again and have embarked in the process of healing.

Grandma and Gloria gave me the love and support I needed to start my journey of healing, but I learned that I needed, at least temporarily, to be alone to complete it—that I had nothing to give to anyone until I got the basics under my belt. It has taken me almost a lifetime to realize that you must be grounded in a comprehensive understanding of yourself, truth, and God's love before your foundation is rock solid, and what grows from that solid foundation can't be shaken.

My first step was to stop acting like a foster child in a new home, wearing my mask, and hoping that people would like me enough to keep me. I started looking at my difficulties one by one. Listening to others has always been a challenge for me. I catch myself interrupting before other people have completed their thoughts. For a long time, I wasn't aware of how often I did this, how annoying it is, or how I looked to others. I just knew that people seemed to shut down after they talked with me a while. I came to realize that this habit was out of fear of being still, close and silent with people. Ever since I can remember, I've been afraid of silence. It was very silent when my mother left, and I never wanted to hear that again.

Another aspect of my interpersonal challenge stems from my Attention Deficit Disorder (ADD). It isn't unusual for me to get distracted during conversations and then start rambling, moving way beyond the initial point I intended to make. Because I've had ADD all my life, I believed that the disrupted thoughts and the associated behavior, which have had devastating effects on my relationships and on how people perceive me, were my burden alone. Only recently have I learned, through group therapy, that ADD has played a bigger role than I first suspected in making me feel so disconnected from others. There is so much more to the condition than what most of us hear in sound bites. The image of ADD, often confused with ADHD (Attention Deficit Hyperactivity Disorder), is of a hot-wired kid bouncing off the walls. But the reality is that many people with ADD feel so different they don't know how to connect with people, and, at some point, they just stop trying. Many of us medicate this pain, resulting in addictions of some kind. I'm overcoming mine.

My extreme passion in conveying my thoughts or carrying out actions has also been misconstrued. I hadn't realized that this intensity can come across at times as arrogance or insensitivity. When I slip into hyper-focus (another manifestation of ADD), some think I'm being self-absorbed. Realizing that I was missing key social cues increased my belief that I was just screwed up.

I shared the pain of my isolation only with my grandmother; she was the one who saw how hard it was for me to overcome the lingering effects of abandonment and to build meaningful personal relationships. I had survived by putting on different masks so I could give people whatever impression was necessary to be granted opportunities and to be a welcome presence in their lives. Whenever I tried to show my true self, I often lost friends—and even loved ones—who couldn't figure out whether I was Dr. Jekyll or Mr. Hyde and who would cut bait and run. To shield myself from the heartbreaks associated with rejection and disappointment, I built intricate defense mechanisms, locking up my intimate emotions in separate boxes.

Grandma knew all about those boxes—she had some of her own and was trying to break through them, which was what gave her permission to look into my soul. I'm still working on finding the keys to my boxes so I can open them and let in all the people I love.

I'm also trying to drop my masks with my children, to be fully present and engaged in my relationship with them, to experience the beauty of their spirits, and to invite them to do the same with me. I aspire to be a whole person with them. Up until now, I've been able to share only a part of myself with my family. At home, I am the provider and protector—two roles I'm good at. I've played those parts since the age of four. However, I've been afraid to be still and enjoy the moment. To this day, I dread intimate "quality" moments. This inability to open up has hurt Gloria and my children, but especially Gloria. She has been there for me 100 percent, even though I wouldn't let her come really close or wouldn't be as close to her as she needed in return. Somehow, she has always loved me anyway.

I'm sharing all these personal revelations to let people know that wanting to break the cycle is not enough. Learning *how* to do it comes first, and you start that learning by making an honest inventory of your strengths and your weaknesses. Once you see where the gaps are in your life, you can start to fill them.

When you escape your own prison, let yourself become free from your past, and embark on the road to healing your broken spirit; then you are able truly to create a different future for yourself and the people who want to love you. I am learning how to ask for help whenever I need it, and I will keep asking and trying until I am whole.

13

Trouble Don't Last

He was just another baby born
destined for the ghetto cement,
to another teen mom,
given no support, no hope, and no encouragement.
When they wrote him off, they must not have
thought,
that baby boy, someday would walk
among children, mayors, and presidents.
Whoever thought when they passed him by
pretending as if they did not hear his cries,
Someday the baby would become a man,
then work to do everything he can
in search of those with helping hands,
to make this country a better land.
Who would have imagined, the one they rejected
Would find his voice among the abused and
neglected?
Who would have thought out of so much pain
God would give purpose ... and then call him
Shane
There are many little Shanes along your way.
Just stop, look, and listen.
You will hear them say,
"Wake up; don't forget about me; I need you
today.
Without your help, I might go astray.
If you don't look the other way,
You will be proud to know someday
When you got involved, you helped me say
I made it; I did OK.
Then I will rise, and then I will say ...
Because you cared, "trouble didn't last always."

—S. Salter

I remember those tender, innocent feelings I used to have as a little boy, and I remember when I lost them. While I can never make the pain that gets in the way of my intimate relationships go away completely, I can certainly keep working on my day-to-day efforts to manage it. My sole focus at this stage of my life is learning who I am and how to love me. No more pretending to be what I'm not, no more pushing who I am aside. So forgive me when you meet me if you find that I talk a little too much, or if I walk a little too fast, fight a little too hard, and choose to keep company with the underdogs. I'm just a plain ole' guy who's a work in progress, who says what he means and means what he says. Misunderstood and disliked by many, loved by a few, the only way I can truly love my family and others who are important to me is to first know, accept, and love myself.

My grandmother opened this door for me on the day she rocked me in her arms, laid my head on her lap, and simply said, "I know baby; I know." She knew that all my life I just wanted to know what love felt like. I longed to be wanted, understood, and connected—something I lost early, something that all the moving from home to home took away from me. When Grandma said, "I know; I know," I couldn't believe she really did know until I learned her story. Then I suddenly realized that her story was my story, and my pain was our common understanding. Light bulbs started flashing as I looked in her eyes and saw all the years of heartache, disappointment, and broken dreams riding heavy on her back.

Grandma's pain had become her poison, and she was imprisoned by it. But the gates opened for both of us, and our opportunity for healing unfolded. I opened my heart wide, and love came dancing into my soul for the very first time. She struggled, trying to give what she thought was love to her children, only to realize in so many ways that what she gave was not what they needed most. Until recently, I was doing the same thing. Fortunately, I have the chance to continue working on the path to healing and recovery. Grandma doesn't.

My grandmother died on Christmas Eve a few years ago. She was taken to a hospital in New York where they found a malignancy on her kidney. For reasons I never did understand, her daughter,

Jewel, didn't want me there and encouraged others in the family not to call me. However, Grandma's best friend, Linda, knowing that my grandmother would want to see me, did call us, although not until it was too late. Gloria took the call (I was at a shopping mall) and got the sad news that Grandma wasn't doing well.

"She's been in the hospital all weekend," Linda told my wife. "She's tired after the surgery just last month, and I think she's really ready to go."

"What do you mean?" asked Gloria in disbelief. "How could she just give up?"

"I'm telling you, it doesn't look good," came the reply. "She asked for papers about no more procedures or something like that. A whole bunch of doctors then came into the room, asking her all kinds of questions. 'What's your name? Who's the President? What year is it?' Know what I mean?"

"Yes," said Gloria who understood that the doctors were trying to determine if she was of sound mind when she refused further intervention by signing an order not to resuscitate.

"Even after they told her she would be dead in hours if she didn't go on dialysis," continued Linda, "she said no. Shane has to get here. I wasn't supposed to call him because of you-know-who, but that ain't right, and I just couldn't let this go down like that."

While thanking Linda and telling her how grateful I would be for her call, Gloria started to sob. It had been only a few years since her adoptive mother had died—by a strange coincidence also around Christmas—and Grandma had been her strength, helping her through it, tiptoeing around, but keeping a watchful eye. Gloria just couldn't believe that our family was facing another devastating loss in such a short time. She remembered all the good times she had shared with Grandma over the years, their private talks, and their soap opera updates.

Brittney and Courtney came downstairs and saw Gloria's weeping. Brittney, our nurturing child, immediately asked what was wrong. When Gloria told them to sit down, Courtney, our child who says whatever comes to mind, blurted out, "Did someone die or something?" Little did know how close to the truth her perception was. When Gloria told them that Grandma Salter was in the hospital and was not going to make it, at first they couldn't believe it.

Brittney, in dismay, mentioned she was going to miss Grandma's cooking. Courtney followed, saying she would miss Grandma's infamous one-liners. And then she started quoting them:

"You'd have to be Ray Charles not to see that." (When someone tried to pull a fast one.)

"Leave this old lady alone; I'm not losing any weight. Let me tell you: don't nobody want a bone but a dog!" (When I urged her to lose weight.)

"Give me my flowers while I'm here, not when there's a tag on my toe." (About postponing love, reward, or praise.)

"This family is dysfunctional with a capital D!" (Whenever someone did something crazy in New York.)

Gloria called me on my cell phone and told me about Grandma's condition. I sprinted for the train station. I could barely see straight. On the train, my phone rang again. It was Jewel, informing me that grandma had gone "peacefully with everyone by her bedside as she took her final breath." *Everyone except me,* I thought. All I could do was moan and cry out, "No, no, no."

"Trust me; it was beautiful, Shane," Jewel said. "She was ready to go home. She left with a smile like she saw something and her last word—I couldn't believe it—was 'Hallelujah!' "

I felt that she was rubbing in the fact that I had missed being there—that it was a call meant more to convey spite than anything else. Since then, I've tried to come to terms with that sad experience by rationalizing that Jewel and the others may have needed that time with Grandma more than I did.

I often teased Grandma by begging her not to leave me behind to deal with her daughter's drama and the rest of the family when she died. However, I meant it when I told her, "If you happen to leave first, count on the fact that, after I put your remains in the ground, the relationships I have with the rest of this family will be buried as well. I won't let them do to me what they've done to you." She heard me quietly, and—although I know she did not agree—she certainly understood.

Because our relationship had been so close, I was sure that during her final hours and at her funeral, I wouldn't feel like an outsider from foster care. Yet, the way my family in New York was treating me sent a powerful message and almost made me feel that way again. I knew Gloria and all of my children were grieving, especially David, who was very close to Grandma himself. I focused on the goal and remained strong for everyone.

When I arrived at the hospital in the Bronx, I learned that Grandma's body had already been taken down to the morgue. I told them I was the executor and asked to be taken to the morgue to say good bye. I wasn't sure that I was really ready, but I felt calm, as if she and I were doing this thing together. I walked in and saw my grandmother's body, her skin smooth as silk. At first, I just stared. Then the orderly said, as he left to give me privacy, "I've never seen a body this peaceful down here; she has no hint of strain or stress on her face."

I stroked Grandma's cheek. It was a little cold, but not so cold that I couldn't tell that it was only recently that she had departed on her journey home. While I was sad that she was gone, I was happy to see her at peace. It was clear to me that the pain and heartache that consumed her when she lived were over. Her tasks were done, and she appeared to be at rest.

I simply said to her, "Now you can get the peace you were unable to find here on earth. Just tell my mother for me that I love her and miss her love every day. I don't know how I will get through this, Ma. I don't know how I will go on without you? Who will I turn to when I need to talk late at night. Who will I call from the car during those long drives to and from home, burning countless cell phone minutes? No one understood me like you did."

And then I made her a promise: "Ma, I will get through this. I will be strong, and I will be patient with Jewel. I'll hold my tongue until this is over and be strong for Pierre too. Thank you for loving me," I added, "Thank you for showing me what love *really* is; thank you for believing I could do anything, even when I thought otherwise." Finally, I sang *Mama* from "Boyz to Men," off the *Big Mama* soundtrack, "Mama, you know I love you, Mama, you're the queen of my heart. Mama, loving you is like food to my soul." I then kissed her gently on the forehead one last time and said good bye. I like to think she felt that kiss.

My grandmother had been my strength and my pride; she had helped take my loneliness away. Now, like all the others who had journeyed down this road and suffered this kind of loss, I had to find a way to survive. But that's where my faith came in. I knew I would make it because God promises that although weeping may endure for a night, joy will come in the morning. "Trouble don't last always."

Because it was Christmas and no arrangements could be made for a few days, I got on Amtrak and went back to D.C. in a daze. While I was on the train, I remembered that everything in my life happened for a reason, and I decided that my grandma had probably arranged it so that she and I had our private time for closure just the way it played out. We had created a very special relationship, and it ended in a very special way that was just for us. However, I couldn't help but also think that this was going to be yet another miserable holiday season. Gloria's mom died December 9, my mother died December 16, and Robbie and my grandmother died December 24. How do you ever experience a happy Christmas again with those kinds of losses during the holidays?

When I returned home, I anxiously tried to track down KB. Finally, I found Ma Mills in Richmond at her daughter Joni's house, and she agreed to relay the news to KB. But I still had not come to terms with Grandma's death.

Alone in my Capitol Hill apartment, the reality was beginning to hit me—my grandmother and best friend was really gone. I lost my appetite, I couldn't sleep, and I couldn't keep still. I wasn't

able to let Gloria and the kids help me, and my best male friend
was away for Christmas. Luckily, my friend Reese stopped by. He
quickly realized what a hard time I was having, that I couldn't
seem to jump-start my usual family patriarch role, and couldn't
start any task related to planning Grandma's funeral. Reese called
around, got help, and carried me through it. We sat together and
planned Grandma's service according to her expressed wishes.

Ironically, the only other time I had been this vulnerable and in
this much pain was when I lost my job at the Freddie Mac
Foundation on Grandma's birthday. The big difference was that
Grandma was there to see me through it and to remind me I'd been
through rougher seas and crossed too many bridges to let myself
think my ship was gonna sink now. This time I had to trust that, in
my time of need, I wouldn't be left hanging. I always knew that
Grandma would not walk away, and if I stumbled, grown man or
not, she would be there to catch me and to keep me from hitting
the ground. This time, I would have to work through things the
best way I knew how—in silence and alone. Perhaps having had
Grandma's support through the pain, rejection, and humiliation
when I lost my job had prepared me for what I would eventually
call a one-two-three-punch.

I went back up to New York and finished the rest of the
arrangements. There, Pierre let me know he would not be coming
to his mother's funeral. When I asked him why, he said that he
couldn't stand being in the same space as his sister. He came to the
funeral home and said good bye to his mother before the service;
then he left. It was a shame, but I accepted his wishes.

It was frustrating that all of those loving family members who had
cried and carried on at her bedside were not around to help now.
Only my sister Shanique and my cousin Omar (also shunned by
the family during Grandma's final hours) were brave enough to
accompany me as I tried to deal with Jewel and to arrange
Grandma's funeral.

Although it felt like going to the gas chamber, I was committed to
ensuring the noneventful, home-going service my grandmother
deserved. And that meant being extraordinarily kind to Jewel,
even driving her back and forth in my car. To increase my

tolerance level and manage my temperament, I decided to have a memorial service for Grandma at our family church outside of D.C. in Reston, Virginia, where she had occasionally visited. That way, no matter what went down in New York, I knew Grandma would have a spirit-filled, drama-free tribute.

The morning of the funeral felt like a day I had dreaded all of my life. I wanted to get through it as quickly as possible. We were all afraid that Jewel would make a scene, so Shanique and I walked next to her, each of us holding one of her hands. Gloria and the children were right behind me. Jewel didn't make a scene—but then she had already struck.

Before the service even began, Jewel stole the silver plate inscribed with Grandma's name out of the coffin! When I pointed it out to Shanie, my sister said, loud enough for everyone to hear, "Unbelievable. Stealing out of the coffin! Unbelievable. Robbing the dead. I've seen it all!" Although I too was disgusted by Jewel's action, my sister's uncontrolled outburst almost caused me to burst out laughing.

All I could do was pray, "Dear Lord, just get me through this." My worst fear was that a fight would break out, someone would knock over Grandma's casket, her body would roll out of the church onto the street, and hair weaves would be flying everywhere—the makings of a Salter "made-for-TV" movie directed by Spike Lee for sure. I wonder what we would have called it? We got through the service without any more drama, thank goodness.

Planning the funeral, riding in the limousine directly behind the hearse, and being my Grandma's executor somehow erased all the leftover pain from the rejection and abandonment I experienced in my childhood. I no longer felt illegitimate. This was my family, for better or worse. No longer did I have to try on someone else's last name or change my first name in search of a new identity.

I again reflected on that Jennifer Holiday song, "And I'm telling you, I'm *not going* ... you're gonna *love me*." Well, Grandma did love me and, for once, I didn't seek and then run from love. I looked it straight in the eye and said, "Love, I am here, ready as I was the day I took my first breath. Give me the best you got. There is no turning back now. Never again will I run from love; never again will I run from me."

I am a Salter: Shane Lenard Rico Salter Sr.—the great-grandson of Richard Sawyer; the first grandchild of Sandra Ethelyn Sawyer-Salter; the first son of Sharon Elaine Salter; and the father of David Lenard, Tiffany Monique, Shane Rico, Brittney Nicole, Courtney Shanade, Moyé Jordan, and Nigel Keith. My great-grandfather, my grandmother, and my mother were the people whose living gave me the song I sing, as captured by the chapter titles in this book. And I reflected on all of what my life meant while preparing to bury Grandma.

Although I was just "one more baby child born" in the South Bronx, "I dreamed" of a day when I would start feeling that I was human and that I belonged to "a family." Deep in my heart, I always knew someday I'd find the "dream with my name on it" and then "the storm would be over." I never imagined that I'd get married, have children, and melt like butter when I hear them say they "love Daddy." But I always believe, no matter who rejected or discarded me, that my "Change Is Gonna Come."

The genuine love between me and my grandmother emerged through forgiveness, hope, and healing, and it ultimately gave us "Our Song." She took the little boy who became a man and made sure he learned that none of us is perfect and that many of the mistakes families make are often rooted in generational cycles of ignorance and pain. Hearing "you were always loved" from great-granddad and Grandma had a transformational effect on my life and contributed greatly to my healing.

Now, because of love and forgiveness, "Still I Rise." I rise each day hoping others will understand "Why I Sing" this testimony to other children, families, and leaders. It has become evident that when this child became a four-year-old-parent, "Trouble Did Not Last." The four-year-old parent became a man who learned he was "Born for This"—born to sing tears into a smile and hatred into love.

I now know that I don't need to beg for acceptance, understanding, or love. In the reality of that moment, as I looked over grandma's coffin, I believed that she was finally at rest, and it dawned on me that my task was almost complete. Now my final expression of love was to escort her body to the cemetery without the conflict and drama that had plagued our family for generations. While making the funeral arrangements for grandma, I found closure for everything that was denied me at my mother's death. As Grandma requested, the procession of limousines and cars followed the hearse to Fairlawn Cemetery, where she would join Uncle Leroy and my mother.

When we arrived at the cemetery and I had signed the papers authorizing the plot to be opened, there was no denying my legitimacy. I was the family patriarch and the only one to whom Grandma could entrust her final arrangements. Life is full of strange twists, isn't it?

As I got out of the limousine, I knew there were many people there, but my misty eyes stopped me from seeing them clearly. Tremors caused my cold hands to shake uncontrollably. I could not bear to see the sadness in the faces of my wife and children as we gathered at the gravesite. The grave handlers asked if I wanted to watch the lowering of the coffin. Without hesitation, I said, "Yes." I couldn't help but look into the grave and try to see my mother's coffin: this was the closest I had been to her since I was four years old. A part of me wanted to jump into the grave and put my arms around the box that held her remains.

I realized that I still mourned and ached for my mother. It was ironic that, all of my life, I had tried everything to fill the gaping hole that her absence left in my heart. Its depth was mirrored only by the size of this gravesite. The one who had helped me fill that hole was now about to fill the one before me. My grandmother was the only person I had learned to love authentically, and now I was watching her coffin being lowered on top of the coffin occupied by the body of the woman I long every waking day to see again, the one who gave me life.

When the funeral director and minister were done, I hugged various family members as we all walked to cars and designated limousines. My driver knew the plan. The limousine that Gloria, the kids, and I had ridden in was going back empty to New York.

My son David had driven the family up from Virginia in our SUV and had brought it to the cemetery in New Jersey. I wanted to leave for Washington straight from the cemetery and not spend one minute more than necessary with the toxic members of Grandma's family. Once she was in the ground, we jumped in the Yukon and headed for home. I left the cemetery and never looked back, just as I had told Grandma I would.

With David at the wheel, shortly after we got onto the New Jersey Turnpike, I opened the letter my grandmother had left for me in the box with her burial papers. I had distributed the letters she had left for other members of the family, as instructed, but had waited to read mine until the service was over.

We had often talked about death, and Grandma and I had always agreed that, when either of us went, there should be no "boo-hooing" or "falling out" over the casket because all of our love had been expressed while we lived. We never let a conversation end without saying "I love you," or a visit end without a big mushy hug and kiss. We laughed and told each other everything, so that was supposed to be enough to get me through all of this. But I should have known Grandma would somehow find a way to have the last word. Her final letter to me is copied as she wrote it.

Hi Darling:

I know that this is a sad time for you, You know baby, that you are my first grand-child, my best friend, we could talk & say anything to each other, I love you & have loved you, more then you will ever know, but you have known that, you know that you are my baby & you have given me so much joy, You have made me so proud of you. Also, you gave me my flowers when I was around, all the time, never was there ever anything, that even you thought I wanted or needed that you didn't make it possible, Ahme I love you so much, I haven't left you, just look & you will see me smile, One day we will be together again, I'll always be around you the bond is there & it always will be. When you play that song Precious Lord, think of me, think of me when you made me laugh, & when you said silly things to me, Be strong, take care of your-self & family I love you so much. Love you,

"Mom"

There is no amount of money or inherited material possessions that could have brought me the comfort and peace of mind of her last letter. When she first started coming to visit me, Grandma did not attend a church and her faith was weak, to say the least. Through our relationship with Gloria and the family, she also developed a relationship with our pastor, attended church regularly, and clearly asked in her final hours of life for God to forgive her for any wrong she had ever done. I was so glad to hear that my grandmother's last word was "Hallelujah!"

As I look over my life—at all my past journeys and all the possibilities that lie ahead—I realize that there is no ending point. I will continue to grow and evolve as long as I live. I want my life to be complete and balanced, I want to continue healing, and I want my family to be as healthy as we can be. I now realize this process will take time and more work.

◆   ◆   ◆

Where are they now?

KB and I don't have much of a relationship. It's sad: we were inseparable as kids until he was twelve and I was fifteen. Now, we are more like Cain and Abel. After numerous failed attempts to work out our problems, I've let him go. Our bond has fallen victim to our experience, but who knows what could happen in the future. I respect him for all that he has endured and accomplished and for fighting the good fight.

My sister Shanique lives in New York with her beautiful son, my nephew Shalik. I'm so proud of the woman she's become, and we have a healthy relationship.

My brother David went to technical school and became a certified cable installer. David has worked for Verizon for more than six years. He and his wife own their own home in Maryland. I can't help but chuckle as I watch him repeatedly open his doors to relatives and friends down on their luck—a chip off the old block, if I do say so myself. Unfortunately, three months after Grandma was buried, David was involved in a tragic, head-on collision. The threat of losing my brother right after my grandmother almost pushed me to the deep end. It was touch and go for a while, but David continues to recover.

My oldest son, David, serves in the Army National Guard, is certified as an EMT, and works for a major hotel chain in Arlington, Virginia. He has a healthy relationship with his birth father and sisters, along with his former foster father.

Tiffany, my firstborn, returned to New York for school, works for the Arts Council, and is currently raising her former partner's child. She has accepted her mother's limited capacity to deliver on promises and to fully engage with her in a nourishing relationship. As expressed in a rap CD she recorded and gave to me, Tiffany recognizes how much it took as a teen father to step up to the plate, remain there, and ensure her needs were met. As a result, she has forgiven me for my past mistakes and loves me unconditionally.

Tara, Tiffany's mom, is raising her toddler in New York. Three of her sons were returned from an emergency foster home several years ago and live with their father in Hilton Head, South Carolina.

Shane-Rico, my first son through adoption, lives in his New York apartment not far from Tiffany. He is enjoying bachelorhood, works on information technology, and through a supervised process over the past few years, recently transitioned off all medication.

Aunt Cookie's son, Omar, is working for the Department of the Treasury in Washington, D.C. He is a wonderful, committed father of four children and an inspiration to his brother and sister.

The Moragnes, my unofficial foster parents, have retired and now live in Greenwood, South Carolina. It was Dad Moragne, in fact, who inspired me to share this journey with the public as an opportunity for learning and healing. He thought that after all I had gone through, just graduating from high school was a miracle. He told me, "You're supposed to do something with all of this. Write it down. People need to know about it." Although I was only seventeen when he said those words, I promised him I would write a book some day, and now that promise is fulfilled.

Reverend Kennedy relocated to Washington, is adopting two more children, and plays an active role in my life as friend, Dad, and as Grandpa to my children. We have a great adult relationship. He is a complex, yet straightforward person. I understand him much better now, and I love him for his heart and the sincerity of his intentions. What we were unable to have when I was a kid, we are enjoying twofold as adults.

I never saw Mr. Pointer again. I have searched for him. People I've met on the speaking circuit have also offered to search for him in all kinds of creative ways. After all the heartache I caused him and all the time he invested in me, I wish he could have seen the man I've become. He was a powerful social worker with a profound effect on my life.

For the longest time I thought that the trouble I went through while growing up just required me as an adult to live in my own world as if everything were okay. Then a voice inside me said that there was a purpose for my pain. When I asked what that purpose could be, the voice led me to transformational healing. I then understood and answered the calling to share my experience with others so we could all open locked doors of hope and healing.

I believe that we each have a purpose for being here. It is my living testimony that the lives discarded as trash, God means for treasure, and that the voices others want to silence, God makes sure are heard. Every child has potential, and every child must be valued. Sadly, many of our children have so much deep-rooted pain that it has become a prison locking up their potential. They cannot find their life's purpose, and they feel devalued by their community and our nation.

The consequence to society for ignoring that pain is incalculable. You don't have to go far to see how angry many of our children are at adults because adults have not responded to their basic needs. We must do better for all of our children—at the very least for those in harm's way. Through our actions, we must let them know that winds may rise and storms may blow, but "Trouble Don't Last Always!"

Epilogue

Born for This

Life doesn't mean just happiness,
there's always room for rain,
but if we learn what autumn knows,
spring will come again.
Let's celebrate each moment of our lives.
If we ever lose our way
because the heart is torn,
never let it question why
the reason we were born.
Born for this, destined for greatness,
I was prepared for this,
By learning with love there comes a risk,
and in my quest to find the answer,
found I was born for this.

—S.Mills

Unfortunately, child abuse continues to be a national problem and poses many challenges for our communities, the child welfare system, and the medical and legal structures. It's not someone else's problem—it's everybody's problem.

We can no longer allow ourselves to think that kids in the system are "just trouble." They are children, like yours, who need a kind word, a loving gesture, and a helping hand. You may be the one who can change their lives forever.

I think we should alter our strategy and invest the bulk of our dollars in supporting and keeping high-risk families together, thereby preventing kids from entering the foster care system if at all possible. Pilot programs in Washington, D.C., and other cities around the nation demonstrate that this prevention can be done. We need to take aggressive action to break the cycle of abuse, neglect, and lack of parenting. We must establish easily accessible, comprehensive, residential and nonresidential programs that support the family unit, engage the community, are culturally sensitive and competent, and address both parenting skills and health issues.

Over the years, I've seen how government youth-welfare decisions and policies re-victimize children and perpetuate their troubles. Officials set policies and program directions without getting input from their clients' communities or the children they serve—and then they wonder why those programs fail. But that's changing. A few years ago the San Diego chapter of CASA launched a program called "Voices for Children," which was specifically designed to give foster kids input into the system. The Jim Casey Youth Opportunity Initiative also helps children have some say in their care in several communities, and child welfare administrators across the country are beginning to include foster youth in program reform.

Although this change is certainly encouraging, the question of what happens to children when they leave foster care at age eighteen is still unaddressed. Most kids who age out of the system are completely unprepared for the challenges they will face on their own. Services to support them either do not exist or are not coordinated properly.

The system's revolving door leaves most of its "graduates" more abused and neglected than they were before arriving, with limited capacity to engage in healthy relationships, with few job skills, and with no one to turn to for support. Research indicates that 33 percent of homeless people and 80 percent of our prison population were once in foster care. The numbers are equally alarming when it comes to those in mental health institutions. Far too many children can't beat those depressing odds on their own, but the presence of caring adults could get them over life's hurdles.

The tragedy is that there is no yardstick that the public can use to measure the relative success or failure of those entrusted with raising victimized children. It's astonishing to think that we apply higher accountability standards to our car mechanics than to child-welfare administrators. I don't think anyone would keep sending a new BMW or Land Rover to the same auto shop if it came back inoperable or more damaged than when it was taken in for service.

Why, then, would any reasonable, tax-paying citizen tolerate a system in which the children removed from families where abuse or neglect occurred are further traumatized in foster care through multiple moves or—even worse—are re-victimized through sexual, emotional, and physical abuse?

Because child-welfare agencies do such a poor job of preparing youth for adulthood, I think that foster-care children should be guaranteed life-long benefits comparable to those provided (and rightly so) to our military veterans. They too are veterans, but of a different kind of war. The act of removing a child from his or her home implies a permanent commitment on the part of the government to that child's welfare. How does anyone in good conscience dare to remove children from their families without ensuring that the caretakers can provide those children with a brighter future that maximizes their potential?

According to a recent study released by Casey Family Programs and Harvard Medical School, adults who were formerly in foster care have up to twice the rate of Post-Traumatic Stress Disorder

(PTSD) as U.S. war veterans.[1] Although opinions differ regarding entitlement programs, providing services for our foster-case, graduates is not only morally right, but investing in such services is economically sound when compared to the cost of long-term institutionalization in mental health facilities or prisons—the end of the line for many of the victims of a failed system.

I invite you to join me in motivating our political leaders to pass legislation that gives children raised in foster care the following:

1.   Lifetime access to excellent mental health services. Because many of the mental health problems found in foster children (such as PTSD, depression, and drug addiction) are also seen in soldiers returning from combat,[2] the military or veterans' healthcare facilities could be used to treat mental health issues that can emerge at any time in the lives of victims of neglect or child abuse.

2.   Lifetime access to educational benefits that cap at a reasonable dollar amount. This plan will enable former foster-care children to complete their education when they are mentally and emotionally mature, instead of mandating that eighteen-year-olds to immediately leave the system with the expectation that they are equipped and disciplined to further their education based solely on their chronological age.

3.   The same home-ownership benefits that veterans receive. This plan would apply, provided that the applicants meet the financial and credit criteria.

4.   Supportive housing, similar to half-way houses, during times of crisis that results from unstable living conditions, poor   mental   health,   limited   education   and

---

[1] P.J. Pecora, R.C. Kessler, J. Williams, K. O'Brien, A.C. Downs, D. English, E. Hiripi, C.R. White, T. Wiggins, & K. Holmes, 2005. "Improving Family Foster Care: Findings from the Northwest Foster Care Alumni Study," Seattle, WA: Casey Family Programs. Available at www.casey.org

underemployment. Most of us can rely on our families as a safe haven throughout our lives and to provide support during difficult times; most foster care veterans don't have that option.

5.   Greater accountability of guardians and mental health providers to ensure they promote conflict-resolution and problem-solving skills while children are in foster care. When things become difficult in a foster family, the family often abandons the child instead of working the problem through. This abandonment means that foster children rarely learn how to resolve conflict or to maintain relationships. Caregivers must help abused and neglected children work through the issues that this kind of trauma creates. If children of abuse and neglect are encouraged to live in the present and to develop the tools that provide healing from their pain, then I believe they will have a better chance to discover the purpose of their lives and to find the motivation to make their dreams come true.

But legislation is not enough. Religious leaders, congregations, sororities, fraternities, and all civic-minded groups must embrace and provide basic support for youths who are transitioning from foster care back to their communities. A safe place to stay during semester breaks and letters of encouragement or care packages while attending college, are just a few examples of how we can provide encouragement. Thus, we contribute to breaking cycles of abandonment, abuse, and neglect.

It is critical that those who work with a child identified as a "youth at risk" must first believe and hope in all that is possible and then must visualize a bright future for that child—just as most birth parents dream for their own children. Too many children have caretakers who act as though the children's current circumstances have set in stone their fate. I'm glad my survival enabled me to stand witness that this predestination theory is not fact.

If all you can do is look the other way and say, "Um, Um, Um, I know where he'll end up," then you may be contributing to the circumstances and belief systems that cause "him" to end up there. I once interviewed for a position at a renowned medical institution located in Baltimore, Maryland that provides therapeutic foster care and a host of other comprehensive services for special needs children. After completing my interviews with a licensed clinical social worker, a psychiatrist, and three other members of the executive management team, I withdrew my name from consideration as a finalist, because once they learned I was a foster child, they all asked me (with different variations) how I had made it. While there is nothing fundamentally wrong with that question, it became clear that they didn't believe my professional accomplishments were something children in foster care were really capable of achieving.

Children still need today what I needed when I was a child: the support of caring, committed adults who believe in their possibilities. I also needed well-qualified professionals to help me resolve conflicts and build attachments so that in the future I could engage in nurturing, long-term relationships, instead of constantly running from or sabotaging good connections. The system should worry less about whether newly emancipated foster children have an apartment, and should focus instead on ensuring that they have the social and psychological skills necessary for a healthy adult life. Without such skills, when the going gets tough the apartment will be abandoned, and the kids will cut and run instead of seeking support and resolving their problems.

As the old folks use to say, let me make it plain: if you think they *won't* make it, they'll feel your vibe and probably won't. If you believe they *can* make it, they'll feel your vibe and probably will. If you *teach* and show them how to make it, they'll develop the confidence to make it, and yours will be a job well done.

I hope you see that mine has been an incredible journey through trouble and triumph. The true blessing is that, although I have been scorned and covered with scars, I am still strong, determined, and full of courage. All of my life, I've been up against tough odds. My determination to make it to the finish line is fueled by the effect that a terrible multigenerational legacy of drugs, neglect, and abuse has had on my family. Moreover, discovering my own potential to achieve and rise above that trouble legacy, coupled with the ability to forgive and seek forgiveness for mistakes made, is reflective of my core beliefs and the one message that I hope you take from this story: we are not our mistakes; we are our possibilities.

I also hope this message of hope and healing will encourage you to rethink how best to respond to children and families in crisis. Perhaps you will now become determined to remove the biggest obstacle to achieving your personal greatness just as I did by reconciling with my grandmother and by nurturing the love between us. I know I have made progress, but I am still uncertain that I can break the cycle. In fact, sometimes it feels as if I'm repeating it. My internal struggle is ongoing; however, I will never stop trying.

Sometimes, it feels as if I'm living somebody else's life. It's hard to believe that, in one lifetime, this man named Shane was a child in search of the love and the security that a family brings. It's also hard to believe that I have been a teenage parent, a single parent, and, now, an adoptive and birth parent. How did I ever grow up to lead one of the larger foster-care agencies in Washington, D.C.; to run corporate foundations; and to serve as a political appointee?

Life seems to have come full circle. Now, as the CEO of CASA for Children of D.C., an organization that trains volunteers to advocate for abused and neglected children, my experiences build on each other as I try to focus the public's attention on the threats compromising the mental and emotional health and development of children and try to develop strategies that will strengthen families.

Although much has been accomplished over the years, there is still a long way to go before all of America's children can achieve their full potential. Once they enter the foster care system, children are moved from home to home, which is why it is so important for the family and the community to act quickly to keep children out of the foster care system whenever possible. If children must enter the system, then a culturally competent CASA (Court-Appointed Special Advocate) must ensure that they do not "slip between the cracks." Perhaps a culturally competent CASA from the South Bronx or a surrounding area would have identified resources for the treatment my mother needed, and if she had chosen not to accept that support, would have expedited the process of terminating her parental rights. Granted things were different then and, even today, not every CASA is culturally competent, but it would have been an enormous help to have had another set of eyes capable of keeping track of all the players in the system, and who could have supplied information specific to the child, to the system's judges.

I was born to write this book because such solutions are within our grasp. Trouble does not *have* to last always. It takes each of us to be a true neighbor who is willing, in the words of Martin Luther King Jr., "to risk his position, prestige, and even his life for the welfare of others. In dangerous valleys and hazardous pathways, he will lift some bruised and beaten brother to a higher and more noble life." We can all facilitate the healing of abused children and shattered families in our own way. If you can't adopt, be a foster parent. If you can't be a foster parent, be a CASA volunteer, or help out at a neighborhood center. What you get back will be far greater than everything you gave.

Legislative Milestones

The many changes made in legislation since I entered foster care give me reason to remain hopeful that someday all children will be valued and that more families will be supported while raising their children. I have been lucky enough to see my life experience used to influence some of those changes.

My first experience in advocating before Congress was testifying on behalf of the Multi-Ethnic Placement Act (MEPA), along with Rev. Tally of One-Church-One-Child, Rev. Jesse Jackson of the Rainbow Coalition, and Joe Kroll of the North American Council on Adoptable Children. The inter-ethnic adoption provisions of MEPA (amended in 1996) are designed to reduce the length of time children spend in out-of-home care by removing placement barriers against adults whose ethnicity is different from that of the children they want to adopt.

Another important milestone also took place in 1996 when the Temporary Assistance to Needy Families (TANF) came into force as part of the Personal Responsibility and Work Opportunity Reconciliation Act. The goals of TANF are to help low-income families care for their children in their own homes, thereby reducing dependence on public services. It provides job preparation and encourages the formation and maintenance of two-parent families, thus helping to reduce out-of-wedlock pregnancies.

Then came the Adoption and Safe Families Act (ASFA) of 1997, which represented the most significant change in federal child welfare law since the Adoption Assistance and Child Welfare Act of 1980. While ASFA is, above all, committed to making timely decisions to protect children, it also makes reasonable efforts to preserve the family. When I started sharing my experiences in 1989—especially the experience of growing up and aging out of foster care with no family—I dreamed of a law such as this, but never thought it would happen. Had ASFA been in place, my mother might have gotten the help she needed, and the state would have been forced to create a permanent plan for me and my brother within twelve months of our losing our home. Even if my mother had not been able to conquer her addiction, I might have been able to hold onto some of my childhood, and I might have found a loving family and thrived.

One day in a child's life, I feel, is equivalent to a year in the life of an adult. I am glad that now a clock starts ticking as soon as a child is removed from home. Those time limits will help preserve childhoods by forcing professionals to set measurable goals for parents to successfully reintegrate in the lives of their children or to free them for someone else who can. Fortunately, my two youngest sons, Moyé and Nigel, benefited from the spirit of ASFA and became available for adoption at an early age. It is my belief that the tremendous gains they have made are directly attributable to a brief stay in foster care before joining a permanent family and—to give credit where credit is due—to the weekly post-adoption counseling financed by the Freddie Mac Foundation and available for all children adopted through "Wednesday's Child." I think that the longer children remain in foster care, the harder it is to undo the issues that threaten a healthy and happy childhood. As Gloria and I nurture the potential of our two little boys and cultivate their life purpose, I can't stop thinking about all the other children who are also filled with potential and who are equally deserving of the same opportunity.

Success

To laugh often and much;
To win the respect of intelligent people
and the affection of children;
To earn the appreciation of honest critics
and endure the betrayal of false friends;
To appreciate beauty,
to find the best in others;
To leave the world a bit better,
whether by a healthy child,
a garden patch or a redeemed social condition;
To know even one life has breathed easier because
you have lived.
This is to have succeeded.

—Ralph Waldo Emerson

My life purpose has been driven, in part, by a desire to put a face on and give a voice to lives that are filled with purpose and potential and yet are discarded far too often. Inherent is the belief that you can affirm your desire and seek the opportunity to restore hope in children and confidence in families. It is with this purpose that I now sing with jubilation, "Trouble Don't Last Always!" My healing journey began through forgiveness. To be all I hope to be, I now hope to receive forgiveness from family and friends whom I may have hurt, however unintentionally, while on the road to self-discovery, and while learning to function as a healthy partner in relationships. I refuse to let the effects of abandonment, abuse, or rejection, serve as an acceptable justification for me to avoid continuous self-improvement and accountability.

Each day I wake up knowing that my mother, my grandmother, and my great-grandfather lived with a purpose. I have grown determined to succeed in the manner reflected through Emerson's poem. When great-granddad returned my baby shoe and told me I was destined for greatness, his words sent chills down my spine. I didn't know what he meant then, but it sparked a quest to reconcile my troubled journey with my reason for being. Ultimately, I grew to understand that before formed in my mother's womb, my life, like yours, was preordained as a triumphant manifestation of the human spirit and a testament of God's greatness. Overcoming life challenges—with a desire to leave our corner of the world better than we found it—is the greatness of our human experience. When the journey is finally over, I hope to hear, "Well done, thy good and faithful servant."

◆　　◆　　◆

For additional information on CASA, see page 205.

Appendix A

WAKE UP!

The National Scope of the Problem

How many children are abused and neglected in the United States?

Each week, child protective service (CPS) agencies throughout the United States receive more than 50,000 reports of suspected child abuse or neglect. In 2002, 2.6 million reports were filed about the welfare of approximately 4.5 million children.

In approximately two-thirds of these cases, the information in the report was sufficient to prompt an assessment or investigation. Approximately 896,000 children were found to have been victims of abuse or neglect—an average of more than 2,450 children per day.

Approximately four children die every day because of child abuse or neglect (1,400 in 2002). More than half (60 percent) of those 2,450 victims experienced neglect, meaning a caretaker failed to provide for their basic needs. Nearly 20 percent were physically abused, and 10 percent were sexually abused—and these cases are typically the ones that are publicized. The smallest numbers (7 percent) were victims of emotional abuse, which includes criticizing, rejecting, or refusing to nurture a child.

Who is More Likely To Be Abused Or Neglected?

No group of children is immune. Boys and girls are about equally likely to be abused or neglected, and the phenomenon occurs in all races and ethnicities. In 2002, 54 percent of all victims were white, 26 percent were African American, and 11 percent were Hispanic. American Indian or Alaska Native children accounted for 2 percent of victims, and 1 percent were Asian-Pacific Islanders. Children of all ages experience abuse and neglect, but the youngest children are most vulnerable. Children younger than one-year-old accounted for 41 percent of all abuse-related deaths reported in 2002, and 76 percent of those killed were younger than 4.

Who Reports Child Abuse And Neglect?

In 2002, 57 percent of all reports made to CPS agencies came from professionals who came in contact with the abused child (16 percent from teachers; 16 percent from legal, law enforcement, and criminal justice personnel; 13 percent from social service workers; and 8 percent from medical personnel). Many people in those professions are required by law to report suspected abuse or neglect. The other 44 percent of the reports came from nonprofessional sources (such as parents, other relatives, friends, and neighbors), and 10 percent of the reports were anonymous. It is important for everyone to know the signs that may indicate maltreatment and how to report it. We all have a responsibility to keep children safe as we take steps to prevent abuse from occurring in the first place. For more information about recognizing child abuse and neglect, see *Recognizing Child Abuse and Neglect: Signs and Symptoms* on the National Clearinghouse on Child Abuse and Neglect Information website at http://nccanch.acf.hhs.gov/pubs/factsheets/signs.cfm.).*

Appendix B

<u>Statistics on Children and Youth in Care</u>

(All data are for the period ending September 30, 2001, and are taken from the Casey Family Programs' Child Welfare Fact Sheet dated March 15, 2004.)

- 542,000 children and youth are in foster care on any given day in the United States.
- Nearly half of all children in foster care are over the age of 10.
- African American children and children of two or more races are four times more likely than Caucasian children to be placed in out-of-home care.[i]
- Children of color are less likely to be reunified with their birth families.[ii]
- Children of color experience a higher number of placements.
- American Indian and Alaska Native children are three times more likely than Caucasian children to be placed in out-of-home care.

---

*Source: U.S. Department of Health and Human Services, Administration for Children and Families, Children's Bureau. 2004. Child Maltreatment 2002. Washington, DC: U.S. Government Printing Office. Available online at www.acf.hhs.gov/programs/cb/publications/cmreports.htm or by calling the National Clearinghouse on Child Abuse and Neglect Information at (800) 394-3366. Statistics in Child Maltreatment 2002 refer to cases of harm to a child caused by parents or other caretakers; they do not include harm caused by other people, such as acquaintances or strangers.

Emancipation (when a youth in foster care becomes a legal adult)

- Approximately 100,000 youths in foster care are 16 or older.
- Approximately 20,000 youths aged 16 and older make the transition from foster care to legal emancipation each year.

---

[i] Casey Family Programs Child Welfare Fact Sheet: Statistics Illustrating Major Trends and Issues in the Child Welfare System. Calculations derived from data reported in the 2000 Census and 2000 AFCARS.

[ii] Hill, R. 2001." The Role of Race in Parental Reunification." Paper presented at the Race Matters Forum meeting,

Appendix C

Gateways to Information: Protecting Children and Strengthening Families

National Clearinghouse on Child Abuse and Neglect Information
National Adoption Information Clearinghouse

Adult Survivors

The following organizations are among many that have information on adult survivors of child abuse. If you are aware of any others, please contact the Clearinghouse. Inclusion on this list is for information purposes and does not constitute an endorsement by the Clearinghouse or the Children's Bureau.

American Psychological Association (APA)
750 First Street NE
Washington, DC, 20002-
Phone: (202) 336-5500
Toll-Free: (800) 374-2721 URL:
http://www.apa.org/

The American Psychological Association is a national scientific and professional organization representing the field of psychology. The APA offers a wide range of programs and services including a consumer help center, media information, a research office, and a section on public interest topics such as disabilities, ethnic minorities, and issues involving children, youth, and families.

Child Abuse Prevention Network
Email: tom@child-abuse.com
URL:
http://child-abuse.com/capn.shtml

The Child Abuse Prevention Network, originally launched as an outreach effort of the Family Life Development Center at Cornell University, is sponsored by LifeNET, Inc. Through the World Wide Web, the Network provides professionals with online tools and support for the identification, investigation, treatment, adjudication, and prevention of child abuse and neglect.

Childhelp USAB
15757 North 78th Street
Scottsdale, AZ, 85260
Phone: (480) 922-8212
Fax: (480) 922-7061
TDD: (800) 2-A-CHILD
Toll-Free: (800) 4-A-CHILD
URL:
http://www.childhelpusa.org

Childhelp USA is dedicated to meeting the physical, emotional, educational, and spiritual needs of abused and neglected children by focusing its efforts and resources in the areas of treatment, prevention, and research. Its programs and services include the operation of the Childhelp USA National Child Abuse Hotline, residential treatment facilities for severely abused children, child advocacy centers that reduce the trauma of child abuse victims during the interview and examination process, group homes, foster family selection, training and certification, Head Start programs for at-risk children, child abuse prevention programs, and community outreach.

Darkness to Light
247 Meeting Street
Charleston, SC, 29401
Phone: (843) 965-5444
Fax: (843) 965-5449
Toll-Free: 1-866-FOR-LIGHT
(1-866-367-5444) URL:
http://www.darkness2light.org/

Darkness to Light is a primary prevention program whose mission is to engage adults in the prevention of child sexual abuse; to reduce the incidence of child sexual abuse nationally through education and public awareness aimed at adults; and to provide adults with information to recognize and react responsibly to child sexual abuse.

National Clearinghouse on Child Abuse and Neglect Information
330 C Street SW
Washington, DC, 20447
Phone: (703) 385-7565
Fax: (703) 385-3206
Toll-Free: (800) FYI-3366
Email: nccanch@caliber.com
URL:
http://nccanch.acf.hhs.gov

The National Clearinghouse on Child Abuse and Neglect Information, a service of the Children's Bureau, helps professionals locate information on child abuse and neglect and child welfare, fact sheets, resource lists, bulletins, and other publications. Jointly with the National Adoption Information Clearinghouse (NAIC), the National Clearinghouse on Child Abuse and Neglect Information publishes the Children's Bureau Express, an online digest of news and resources for professionals concerned with child maltreatment, child welfare, and adoption.

National Institute of Mental Health (NIMH)
6001 Executive Blvd
Rm. 8184,
MSC 9663
Bethesda, MD, 20892-9663
Phone: (301) 443-4513
Fax: (301) 443-4279
URL: http://www.nimh.nih.gov

The National Institute of Mental Health works to diminish the burden of mental illness through research. NIMH seeks to achieve better understanding, treatment, and eventually prevention of mental illness.

Office for Victims of Crime (OVC)
810 7th Street NW
Washington, DC, 20531
Phone: (202) 307-5983
TTY: (877) 712-9279
Toll-Free: (800) 627-6872
Email: askovc@ojp.usdoj.gov
URL:
http://www.ojp.usdoj.gov/ovc/

The Office for Victims of Crimes was established by the 1984 Victims of Crime Act (VOCA) to oversee diverse programs that benefit victims of crime. OVC provides substantial funding to State victim assistance and compensation programs, the lifeline services that help victims to heal. The agency also supports training designed to educate criminal justice and allied professionals on the rights and needs of crime victims. OVC is one of five bureaus and four offices with grant-making authority within the Office of Justice Programs of the U.S. Department of Justice.

Safer Society Foundation, Inc. P.O. Box 340
Brandon, VT, 05733-0340
Phone: (802) 247-3132
Fax: (802) 247-4233
URL:

The Safer Society Foundation, Inc., a nonprofit agency, is a national research, advocacy, and referral center on the prevention and treatment of sexual abuse. The Foundation provides training and consultation, research, sex offender treatment referrals, a computerized program network, and a resource library. It also publishes materials for the prevention and treatment of sexual abuse.

Sidran Institute
200 East Joppa Road Suite 207
Towson, MD, 21286
Phone: (410) 825-8888
Fax: (410) 337-0747
Email: sidran@sidran.org
URL: http://www.sidran.org/

The Sidran Institute, a leader in traumatic stress education and advocacy, is a nationally focused nonprofit organization devoted to helping people who have experienced traumatic life events. The Institute promotes improved understanding of the early recognition and treatment of trauma-related stress in children, the long-term effects of trauma on adults, and strategies that lead to the greatest success in self-help recovery for trauma survivors. The Sidran Institute also advocates clinical practices considered successful in aiding trauma victims and the development of public policy initiatives that are responsive to the needs of adult and child survivors of traumatic events.

National Clearinghouse on Child Abuse and Neglect Information 330 C St., SW
Washington, DC 20447 (800) 394-3366 or (703) 385-7565

Appendix D

Long-Term Consequences of Child Abuse and Neglect

Factors Affecting the Consequences of Child Abuse

An estimated 903,000 children were victims of child abuse or neglect in 2001 (U.S. Department of Health and Human Services, 2003). While physical injuries may or may not be immediately visible, abuse and neglect can have consequences for children, families, and society that last lifetimes, if not generations.

The impact of child abuse and neglect is often discussed in terms of physical, psychological, behavioral, and societal consequences. In reality, however, it is impossible to separate them completely. Physical consequences (such as damage to a child's growing brain) can have psychological implications (cognitive delays or emotional difficulties, for example). Psychological problems often manifest as high-risk behaviors. Depression and anxiety, for example, may make a person more likely to smoke, abuse alcohol or illicit drugs, or overeat. High-risk behaviors, in turn, can lead to long-term physical health problems such as sexually transmitted diseases, cancer, and obesity.

This fact sheet provides an overview of some of the most common physical, psychological, behavioral, and societal consequences of child abuse and neglect, while acknowledging that much crossover among categories exists.

Physical Health Consequences

Not all abused and neglected children will experience long-term consequences. Outcomes of individual cases vary widely and are affected by a combination of factors, including:

☐   The child's age and developmental status when the abuse or neglect occurred

☐   The type of abuse (physical abuse, neglect, sexual abuse, etc.)

☐   Frequency, duration, and severity of abuse

☐   Relationship between the victim and his or her abuser (Chalk, Gibbons, & Scarupa, 2002).

Researchers also have begun to explore why, given similar conditions, some children experience long-term consequences of abuse and neglect while others emerge relatively unscathed. The ability to cope, and even thrive, following a negative experience is sometimes referred to as "resilience." A number of protective factors may contribute to an abused or neglected child's resilience. These include individual characteristics, such as optimism, self-esteem, intelligence, creativity, humor, and independence. Protective factors can also include the family or social environment, such as a child's access to social support; in particular, a caring adult in the child's life. Community well-being, including neighborhood stability and access to health care, is also a protective factor (Thomlison, 1997).

The immediate physical effects of abuse or neglect can be relatively minor (bruises or cuts) or severe (broken bones, hemorrhage, or even death). In some cases the physical effects are temporary; however, the pain and suffering they cause a child should not be discounted. Meanwhile, the long-term impact of child abuse and neglect on physical health is just beginning to be explored. Below are some outcomes researchers have identified:

Shaken Baby Syndrome. The immediate effects of shaking a baby (a common form of child abuse in infants) can include vomiting, concussion, respiratory distress, seizures, and death. Long-term consequences can include blindness, learning disabilities, mental retardation, cerebral palsy, or paralysis (Conway, 1998).

Impaired Brain Development. Child abuse and neglect have been shown, in some cases, to cause important regions of the brain to fail to form properly, resulting in impaired physical, mental, and emotional development (Perry, 2002; Shore, 1997). In other cases, the stress of chronic abuse causes a "hyperarousal" response by certain areas of the brain, which may result in hyperactivity, sleep disturbances, and anxiety, as well as increased vulnerability to post-traumatic stress disorder, attention deficit/hyperactivity disorder, conduct disorder, and learning and memory difficulties (Perry, 2001; Dallam, 2001).

Poor Physical Health. A study of 700 children who had been in foster care for 1 year found more than one-quarter of the children had some kind of recurring physical or mental health problem (National Survey of Child and Adolescent Well-Being). A study of 9,500 HMO participants showed a relationship between various forms of household dysfunction (including childhood abuse) and long-term health problems such as sexually transmitted diseases, heart disease, cancer, chronic lung disease, skeletal fractures, and liver disease (Hillis, Anda, Felitti, Nordenberg, & Marchbanks, 2000; Felitti, Anda, Nordenberg, Williamson, Spitz, Edwards, Koss, & Marks, 1998).

Psychological Consequences.

The immediate emotional effects of abuse and neglect—isolation, fear, and an inability to trust—can translate into lifelong consequences, including low self-esteem, depression, and relationship difficulties. Researchers have identified links between child abuse and neglect and the following:

Poor Mental and Emotional Health. In one long-term study, as many as 80 percent of young adults who had been abused met the diagnostic criteria for at least one psychiatric disorder at age 21. These young adults exhibited many problems, including depression, anxiety, eating disorders, and suicide attempts (Silverman, Reinherz, & Giaconia, 1996). Other psychological and emotional conditions associated with abuse and neglect include panic disorder, dissociative disorders, attention-deficit/hyperactivity disorder, post-traumatic stress disorder, and reactive attachment disorder (Teicher, 2000).

Cognitive Difficulties. The National Survey of Child and Adolescent Well-Being recently found children placed in out-of-home care due to abuse or neglect tended to score lower than the general population on measures of cognitive capacity, language development, and academic achievement (2003).

Social Difficulties. Children who are abused and neglected by caretakers often do not form secure attachments to them. These early attachment difficulties can lead to later difficulties in relationships with other adults as well as with peers (Morrison, Frank, Holland, & Kates, 1999).

Behavioral Consequences

Not all victims of child abuse and neglect will experience behavioral consequences; however, child abuse and neglect appear to make the following more likely:

Difficulties During Adolescence. Studies have found abused and neglected children to be at least 25 percent more likely to experience problems such as delinquency, teen pregnancy, low academic achievement, drug use, and mental health problems (Kelley et al., 1997).

Juvenile Delinquency And Adult Criminality. A National Institute of Justice study indicated being abused or neglected as a child increased the likelihood of arrest as a juvenile by 59 percent. Abuse and neglect increased the likelihood of adult criminal behavior by 28 percent and violent crime by 30 percent (Widom & Maxfield, 2001).

Alcohol And Other Drug Abuse. Research consistently reflects an increased likelihood that abused and neglected children will smoke cigarettes, abuse alcohol, or take illicit drugs. According to the National Institute on Drug Abuse, as many as two-thirds of people in drug treatment programs reported being abused as children (2000).

Abusive behavior. Abusive parents often have experienced abuse during their own childhoods. It is estimated approximately one-third of abused and neglected children will eventually victimize their own children (Prevent Child Abuse New York, 2001).

Societal Consequences

While child abuse and neglect almost always occur within the family, the impact does not end there. Society as a whole pays a price for child abuse and neglect, in terms of both direct and indirect costs.

Direct Costs. Direct costs include those associated with maintaining a child welfare system to investigate allegations of child abuse and neglect, as well as expenditures by the judicial, law enforcement, health, and mental health systems to respond to and treat abused children and their families. A 2001 report by Prevent Child Abuse America estimates these costs at $24 billion per year.

Indirect Costs. Indirect costs represent the long-term economic consequences of child abuse and neglect. These include juvenile and adult criminal activity, mental illness, substance abuse, and domestic violence. They can also include loss of productivity due to unemployment and underemployment, the cost of special education services, and increased use of the health care system. Prevent Child Abuse America recently estimated these costs at more than $69 billion per year (2001).

Much research has been done about the possible consequences of child abuse and neglect. The effects vary depending on the circumstances of the abuse or neglect, personal characteristics of the child, and the child's environment. Consequences may be mild or severe; disappear after a short period or last a lifetime; and affect the child physically, psychologically, behaviorally, or in some combination of all three ways. Ultimately, due to related costs to public entities such as the health care, human services, and educational systems, abuse and neglect impact not just the child and family, but society as a whole

References Cited

Chalk, R., Gibbons, A., & Scarupa, H.J. (2002). *The multiple dimensions of child abuse and neglect: New insights into an old problem.* Washington, DC: Child Trends. Available online: www.childtrends.org/files/ChildAbuseRB.pdf

Conway, E.E. (1998). Nonaccidental head injury in infants: The shaken baby syndrome revisited. *Pediatric Annals, 27(10),* 677-690.

Dallam, S.J. (2001). The long-term medical consequences of childhood maltreatment. In K. Franey, R. Geffner, & R. Falconer (Eds.), *The cost of child maltreatment: Who pays? We all do.* San Diego, CA: Family Violence & Sexual Assault Institute.

Felitti, V.J., Anda, R.F., Nordenberg, D., Williamson, D.F., Spitz, A.M., Edwards, V., Koss, M.P., & Marks, J.S. (1998). Relationship of childhood abuse and household dysfunction to many of the leading causes of death in adults: The adverse childhood experiences (ACE) study. *American Journal of Preventive Medicine 14(4),* 245-258.

Goldman, J., Salus, M.K., Wolcott, D., & Kennedy, K.Y. (2003). *A coordinated response to child abuse and neglect: The foundation for practice.* Child Abuse and Neglect User Manual Series. Washington, DC: Government Printing Office.

Hillis, S.D., Anda, R.F., Felitti, V.J., Nordenberg, D., & Marchbanks, P.A. (2000). Adverse childhood experiences and sexually transmitted diseases in men and women: A retrospective study. *Pediatrics, 106(1).*

Kelley, B.T., Thornberry, T.P., & Smith, C.A. (1997). *In the wake of childhood maltreatment.* Washington, DC: National Institute of Justice.

Morrison, J.A., Frank, S.J., Holland, C.C., & Kates, W.R. (1999). Emotional development and disorders in young children in the child welfare system. In J.A.

M.W. (Ed.) *Risk and resilience in childhood: An ecological perspective.* Washington, DC: NASW Press.

National Clearinghouse on Child Abuse and Neglect Information. (2001). *In focus: Understanding the effects of maltreatment on early brain development.* Online: http://nccanch.acf.hhs.gov/pubs/focus/earlybrain.cfm. Accessed July 2003.

National Institute on Drug Abuse. (1998). Exploring the role of child abuse on later drug abuse. *NIDA Notes, 13(2).* Online: www.nida.nih.gov/NIDA_Notes/NNVol13N2/exploring.html. Accessed December 2003.

Perry, B.D. (2001). The neurodevelopmental impact of violence in childhood. In D. Schetky & E. Benedek (Eds.), *Textbook of child and adolescent forensic psychiatry.* Washington, DC: American Psychiatric Press. Online: http://www.childtrauma.org/CTAMATERIALS/Vio_child.asp. Accessed February 2004.

Perry, B.D. (2002). Childhood experience and the expression of genetic potential: What childhood neglect tells us about nature and nurture. *Brain and Mind, 3,* 79-100.

Prevent Child Abuse America. (2001). *Total estimated cost of child abuse and neglect in the United States.* Online: www.preventchildabuse.org/learn_more/ research_docs/cost_analysis.pdf. Accessed July 2003.

Prevent Child Abuse New York. (2001). *Causes and consequences: The urgent need to prevent child abuse.* Online: www.pca-ny.org/causes.pdf. Accessed July 2003.

Runyan, D.K., Curtis, P.A., Hunter, W.M., Black, M.M., Kotch, J.B., Bangdiwals, S., et al. (1998). Longscan: A consortium for longitudinal studies of maltreatment and the life course of children. *Aggression and Violent Behavior 3(3),* 275-285.March 2004

Silver, B.J. Amster, & T. Haecker (Eds.), *Young children and foster care: A guide for professionals* (pp. 33-64). Baltimore, MD: Paul H. Brookes.

Silverman, A.B., Reinherz, H.Z., Giaconia, R.M. (1996). The long-term sequel of child and adolescent abuse: A longitudinal community study. *Child Abuse and Neglect, 20(8),* 709-723.

Shore, R. (1997). *Rethinking the brain.* New York: Families and Work Institute.

Teicher, M.D. (2000). Wounds that time won't heal: The neurobiology of child abuse. *Cerebrum: The Dana Forum on brain science, 2(4),* 50-67.

Thomlison, B. (1997). Risk and protective factors in child maltreatment. In Fraser,

U.S. Department of Health and Human Services. (2003) *Child maltreatment 2001.* Washington, DC: Government Printing Office.

U.S. Department of Health and Human Services. (2003). National Survey of Child and Adolescent Well-Being: Baseline report for one-year-in-foster-care sample. Online: http://www.acf. hhs.gov/prog rams/core/ongoing ng_research/afc/exec-sum_nscaw/exsum_nscaw.html. Accessed January 2004.

Widom, C.S. & Maxfield, M.G. (2001). *An update on the 'cycle of violence.'* Washington, DC: National Institute of Justice.

Appendix E

Becoming Part of the Solution
CASA
(Court-Appointed Special Advocates)
for Children

At CASA for Children of the District of Columbia, just like CASA programs all across the United States, we recruit, train, and supervise community volunteers who serve as court-appointed special advocates. Those advocates must meet national standards, and they investigate, recommend to judges, and monitor legal actions that are in the best interests of individual children who are victims of child abuse and neglect.

The goal of CASA is to see that each child is placed as quickly as possible in a permanent home that is safe, nurturing, and free from violence. In a system where dockets overflow and professional caseloads make individual attention challenging, volunteers ensure that the needs of each child are met. By providing objective, detailed information and recommendations to the courts, volunteers help to move the children through the child welfare system and into adoptive families as quickly as possible.

Volunteers, dedicated staff members, and a committed board of directors, work together at this nonprofit youth advocacy agency. CASA volunteers are an ethnically and culturally diverse group. They receive 30 hours of training with experts in the field, and each volunteer is carefully evaluated before being assigned a case.

CASA emphasizes collaboration to ensure that each child will be able to return home or find a new adoptive family. We know that courtroom advocacy, alone, even with hundreds of committed volunteers, will not produce good outcomes. Only widespread community support will enable us to meet the multiple needs of our children, especially for kinship, foster, and adoptive homes.

There are currently more than 900 CASA programs around the country. Get on board and become a part of this movement, which is led by the people for the people. We need more CASA volunteers of color from the communities where the greatest numbers of children enter foster care. We need ordinary citizens who are willing to step up and get to know a child, to make sure that child is never overlooked or forgotten, and to hold their government and themselves responsible for ensuring that children who are abused and neglected have a chance to achieve their full potential and be nurtured as they transition into adulthood. CASA volunteers go into court with their child and help judges make the best possible decision about where their child should live, what school their child should attend, and what educational resources their child needs. They are their child's voice in court. You can perform those crucial services after just 30 hours of training. Our children need us now. So, *do not let another day go by. Put this book down, and call 1-800-628-3223, or visit* www.nationalcasa.org *to find the CASA program near you.*

The national movement to make sure that victims of child abuse or neglect are heard in court began in the 1960s. Judges realized they were making far-reaching decisions about the lives of children without hearing the unique perspectives of those children. Some judges asked social workers or friends to informally investigate child abuse cases and to make recommendations about what would best serve the needs and interests of the child involved.

The first volunteer guardian *ad litem* (GAL) program serving abused and neglected children, was organized by King County Judge David Soukup in 1977 in Seattle, Washington. Word of the success of the King County program spread like wildfire, and similar programs began all over the United States. Because some state statutes require the GAL to be an attorney, the term Court-Appointed Special Advocate (CASA) was coined to describe volunteers from the local community trained to serve as advocates for abused and neglected children involved in juvenile court proceedings. In 1982, the National CASA Association, Inc., was established to serve as an umbrella organization for the growing number of programs in the country. National CASA provides information, technical assistance, research, and training; sponsors an annual national conference; and has a grants program that annually awards millions of dollars to state and local CASA and GAL programs. Membership in National CASA is open to both individuals and programs.

Better Services to Children

- Low CASA caseloads mean complete information about each child, which means that the courts can make better decisions about each child's welfare. CASA volunteers handle just one or two cases at a time and give each child the *sustained, personal* attention he or she deserves.
- Complex cases with multiple risk factors receive more attention so they can move forward in a timely manner.

Without your help, our work cannot be done. Please consider making a generous, tax-deductible contribution to:

CASA for Children of DC
919 18th St., N.W. #510
Washington, D.C. 20006
Att: *Wakeup4Children*
www.casadc.org

Help A Child Now!

Close to 600,000 children are still languishing in the foster care system while waiting for permanent families. They can be school age, teens, or brothers and sisters needing a home together. Some have special physical, emotional, or educational needs. More than 60 percent come from minority cultures. You will find more than 3,000 of those waiting children on the AdoptUSKids website at www.adoptuskids.org.

No child or sibling group in America should have his or her childhood snatched away, and no child should feel that nobody cares. We can do so much better. Please consider becoming a CASA volunteer, mentor, or a foster or adoptive parent. You are a critical part of the solution.

THE END